The Purification of the Soul

Ibn Al-Qayyim

International Islamic Books Publishing House

www.al-Qarni.com

Copyright

TX0008693971

All rights reserved. King Fahd Glorious Quran Printing and the Prophet's Sunnah, peace and blessings be upon him. No part of this book may be reproduced or transmitted in any form or by any means, electronic or mechanical, including photocopying, recording, or by any information storage and retrieval system, without written permission from the Publisher.

"If a rank is decided by Allah for a servant which he could not attain by his deeds, Allah afflicts him with distress in his body or children or wealth, and makes him bear it in patience until he achieves that rank which was written for him."

— Ibn Qayyim al-Jawziyya

Ibn Qayyim al-Jawziyyah's

Ibn Qayyim al-Jawziyyah's name is inseparable from that of his teacher, the 7th / 13th century Hanbali reformer, Ibn Taymiyyah. It is true, in fact, that Ibn Al-Qayyim was the principle compiler and editor of his teacher's writings, and had it not been for him, that voluminous body of work might never have survived. It is also true that Ibn Taymiyyah's point of view had a profound effect on the young man, who at twenty-one years age, became his student and companion.

One of Ibn Al-Qayyim's own students would later write, "Above all, his love for Ibn Taymiyyah was so great that he would never disagree with anything he said. Rather, he supported him in everything and was the one who edited his books and spread his teachings." In fiqh and theology, both men wrote from a Hanbali position, and Ibn Al-Qayyim criticized the same things that his shaykh had so adamantly opposed: innovation (bid'ah), Greek influenced Muslim philosophy, Shi'ism, the doctrine of wahdatu'l-wujud, or 'oneness of being' (attributed to Ibn Arabi) and by extension, the extreme forms of Sufism that had gained currency particularly in the new seat of Muslim power, Mamluk Egypt and Syria.

However, two elements set Ibn Al-Qayyim's writings apart from those of his shaykh. The first is his tone. Ibn Taymiyyah wrote 'with the eye', as it were, and Ibn Al-Qayyim added to that 'the heart'. As a contemporary editor of his works has written, "Although he moved within the sphere of Ibn Taymiyyah's influence, following him in most of his religious rulings, he was more ready than his teacher to be lenient and amiable to those with whom he differed." A typical example of this may be found in his magnum opus, Madarij as-Salikin (The Traveler's Stages), which is a long commentary on a treatise by the 5th / 11th century Hanbali Sufi, 'Abdullah al-Ansari al-Harrawi. Taking exception to something Al-Ansari wrote, Ibn Al-Qayyim prefaced his comments with, "Certainly I love the shaykh, but I love the truth more."

The second is Ibn Al-Qayyim's great interest in Sufism. Some of his major works, such as Madarij, Tariq al-Hijratayn (Path of Two Migrations) and Miftah Dar as-Sa'ada (Key to the Abode of Happiness), are devoted almost entirely to Sufi themes, but this allusions to these themes are found in nearly all his writings. There is no doubt that Ibn Al-Qayyim addressed those interested in Sufism in particular and al-umur al-qalbiyyah - the matters of the heart - in general. In fact, in the introduction to his short book Patience and Gratitude, he states, "This is a book to benefit kings and princes, the wealthy and the indigent, Sufis and religious scholars; (a book) to inspire the sedentary to set out, accompany the wayfarer on the path (as-sa'ir fi't-tariq) and inform the one journeying towards the Goal."

The subjects dealt with by Ibn Al-Qayyim - the way to God, the maladies of the heart, and the virtues - are undoubtedly also those of tasawwuf. Ibn Al-Qayyim's role is, thus, somewhat similar to that of Al-Ghazali (d. 505H / 1111CE) two hundred years before him: to rediscover and restate the orthodox roots of Islam's interior dimension, with the added task of correcting what he saw as new errors that had arisen due to the powerful influence of Ibn Arabi's works. In this sense, he might be descried as a reviver of what he considered to be an authentic inclination of the heart towards Allâh, and the path towards Him.

This is the formula which, in all likelihood, accounts for the ongoing popularity of Ibn Al-Qayyim's works throughout the Arabic speaking world. His thirty or so extant books have been reprinted many times; the principle ones, including the titles cited above, have all been reprinted in both inexpensive and scholarly editions since 1990. The reader who might be attracted to the inner dimension of Islam but not by much of what passes nowadays as Sufism, finds in Ibn Al-Qayyim an exposition of the Way to God, free of 'mythology' or the exclusive terminology of Sufism, written for the generality of believers and with strict insistence upon the main sources of orthodoxy; the Qur'an, the Sunnah, and the practices of the first two generations of Muslims.

"Whoever shows patience and is conscious of Allah (should know) that Allah does not make the reward of those who do good deeds wasted."

— Ibn Qayyim al-Jawziyya

The Life of Ibn Al-Qayyim

Shams ad-Din Muhammad ibn Abi Bakr ibn Qayyim al-Jawziyyah was born in 691H / 1292CE in az-Zur'i, a small village fifty-five miles from Damascus. Little is known of his childhood except that he received a comprehensive Islamic education thanks to the fact that his father was principle of the Madrasah al-Jawziyyah, one of the few centres devoted to the study of Hanbali fiqh in Damascus; hence, the name by which he came to be known: Ibn Qayyim al-Jawziyyah - son of the principle of the Jawziyyah school - or simply, Ibn Al-Qayyim.

After completing his fundamental studies at the Jawziyyah, Ibn Al-Qayyim continued his learning in the circles of the shaykhs who filled the city's mosques. It appears that for some period of time, he came under the influence of Mu'tazili teachings and probably of certain mystics. In the epic-length Ode he wrote in later years, he refers to this period as being one of confusion and misguidance: "All these [ways] did I try, and I fell into a net, fluttering like a bird that knows not where to fly."

This period came to an end in the year 712H / 1312CE, when at twenty one years of age he met the man who would shape his life's orientation in Islam: Taqi ad-Din ibn Taymiyyah. Ibn Taymiyyah had just returned to Damascus from a seven-year stay in Egypt, the last of which he spent under house arrest. His reputation for being an uncompromising defender of the Sunnah and of Hanbali theology was well known to the people of Syria.

Perhaps it was his certitude and strength that appealed to the young Ibn Al-Qayyim, who "like a bird caught in a net, did not know where to fly." In any event, a bond formed between the two men which lasted for 16 years until Ibn Taymiyyah's death.

Between 712H / 1312CE and 726H / 1326CE, Ibn Al-Qayyim married and had three sons - Ibrahim, 'Abdullah and Sharaf ad-Din. He earned his living as teacher and Imam at the Jawziyyah school. His lessons on Hanbali fiqh and his sermons probably showed the strong influence of his teacher for, in 726H / 1326CE, when the authorities of Damascus ordered the arrest of Ibn Taymiyyah and his followers, Ibn Al-Qayyim was among them.

This imprisonment came after Ibn Taymiyyah had been summoned before a council of religious scholars (ulama) for questioning on a point of fiqh: was it permissible for someone visiting the Prophet's - sallAllâhu 'alayhi wa sallam - mosque in Madinah to shorten the prayers? Since the council knew in advance that In Taymiyyah strongly condemned the practise of visiting saint's tombs for the purpose of receiving blessing (tabarruk), they could easily portray his chary answer as proof that he himself propagated a dangerous innovation (bid'ah) by discouraging Muslims form visiting the burial place of their beloved Prophet - sallAllâhu 'alayhi wa sallam. This pretext was used to remove from the public eye a man they regarded as a source of unrest.

The council ruled that Ibn Taymiyyah and all those in Damascus who propagated his teachings - including Ibn Al-Qayyim- should be rounded up and imprisoned in the citadel of the town. Although a few days later the authorities released Ibn Taymîyah's followers, Ibn Al-Qayyim alone chose to stay at the side of his teacher in prison.

Unlike his house arrest in Egypt, during which he was permitted to write and teach his followers, this time Ibn Taymiyyah was not only locked up, but also denied both books and writing materials, a much harder condition for him to bear than prison itself. It has been recorded that during that final imprisonment he would find scraps of discarded paper and write with pieces of charcoal. In 728H / 1327CE, however, having been separated for two years from all those things he had lived for, he passed away. Then and only then did Ibn Al-Qayyim come out of prison to join the multitudes who followed the body of Ibn Taymiyyah to the burial.

It appears that only after his teacher's death did Ibn Al-Qayyim begin his own profile as a writer. This stage of his life was also marked by much travel, learning and teaching, as well as several pilgrimages to Makkah, where he lived for some time.

Our picture of Ibn Al-Qayyim in the last twenty-five years or so of his life is derived mainly from recollections of his two most illustrious students, Ibn Rajab and Ibn Kathir. The latter wrote, "He recited [the Qur'an] beautifully and was loved by a great many people. He neither envied nor harmed anyone, nor tried to find fault with them, nor harboured malice towards them. In short, there were few people like him ... He was dominated mostly by goodness and a virtuous nature."

Ibn Rajab writes, "May Allâh bless him, he was a person of worship and night prayers, someone who used to make prayer last as long as possible; he was devoted to remembrance (dhikr), constant in his love of Allâh, in turning back to Allâh, in seeking forgiveness, in his dependence on Allâh and in humility before Him. He reached a level of devotion which I have never witnessed in anyone else, nor have I seen anyone more vast in learning or more knowledgeable of the meanings of the Qur'an, the Sunnah, and the inner realities of faith. And while I know he was not infallible, yet I have never seen anyone who was closer to the meaning of this word."

In addition to these isolated glimpses of the man, there is evidence that he loved books so much that after his death his sons had to sell off much of his library, keeping only what they themselves could make use of.

Ibn Al-Qayyim died in 751H / 1350CE, when he was scarcely 60 years old. It is recorded that the funeral prayer, attended by many people, was offered at the Umayyad Mosque in Damascus. He was buried a the cemetery of Bab as-Saghir, near the grave of his father - rahimahumAllâh.

"In the case of performing the regular prayers this is due to laziness and love of comfort in its nature, particularly if this attitude is coupled with hardness of the heart, its blockage by sins, inclination to follow desires and mixing with heedless people. With such obstacles at work, the servant will exhibit little interest in performing the prayers. If ever he does perform them he will be doing it reluctantly, with his mind elsewhere, eager to finish it"

— Ibn Qayyim al-Jawziyya

The Second Biography

The Salafi Imam became well-known with the title 'Ibn Qayyim al-Jawziyyah' because his father was the principal of the 'Al-Jawziyyah' school in Damascus. As for his name, it is Shams ad-Din, Abu 'Abdullah, Muhammad the son of Abu Bakr the son of Ayub az-Zura'i (an ascription to Azra' which is in the south of Syria), then Dimashqi, Hanbali.

He was born on the 7th of Safar in the year 691H (1292CE), and was raised in a house of knowledge and excellence. This offered him the chance to take knowledge from the senior scholars of his time, a time when the various sciences of knowledge flourished. He studied under Ash-Shibab an-Nabilisi, Abu Bakr ibn 'Abd ad-Da'im, Al-Qadhi Taqi ad-Din Sulayman, 'Isa al-Mut'im, Fatimah bint Jawhar, Abu Nasr al-Baha' ibn Asakir, 'Ala' ad-Din al-Kindi, Muhammad ibn 'Abdul-Fath al-Ba'labaki, Ayyub ibn Al-Kamal and Al-Qadhi Badr ad-Din ibn Jama'ah.

He took knowledge of the laws of inheritance from Isma'il ibn Muhammad and read the Arabic language to 'Abdul-Fath al-Ba'labaki and Al-Majd at-Tunisi. He studied fiqh with a certain groups of scholars, amongst them being Isma'il ibn Muhammad al-Harrani, and he took 'Usul al-Fiqh from As-Safi al-Hindi. As for his greatest teacher and his shaykh whom he accompanied for seventeen years of his life, and who left the greatest impact upon him - then that is the Imam, the Mujaddid (Reviver), Taqi ad-Din ibn Taymiyyah. Ibn Al-Qayyim took the same methodology as him and traversed his path in waging war against the people of Innovations and Desires and those who deviated from the religion.

As for his own students, then they are many. Amongst them were his son 'Abdullah; Ibn Kathir - the author of Al-Bidayah wa'n-Nihayah; the Imam and Hafidh, 'Abdur-Rahman ibn Rajab al-Baghdadi al-Hanbali - the author of Tabaqat al-Hanabilah; and also Shams ad-Din Muhammad 'Abdul-Qadir an-Nabilisi.

Ibn Al-Qayyim lived in a time in which there was strife and internal confusion and chaos, as well as an external threat which was menacing the Islamic state. For this reason, he used to order with holding fast to the Book of Allâh and the Sunnah of the Messenger, and the rejection of separation and disunity. Amongst his goals was the purging of the religion from the innovations and desires and returning it to its pure and original fountains. So he called for the destruction of the madhhab of blind-following (taqlid), a return to the madhhab of the Salaf and traversing upon their way and methodology. [The last sentence may be understood incorrectly by people, and for a proper discussion as to the manhaj of the salaf regarding taqlid refer to the fiqh section of this site.] Because of this we see that he did not restrict himself to the Hanbali madhhab and often he would take the opinion and view of one of the various madhahib, or sometimes he may have had an opinion which confliucts with the opinion of the all the other madhahib. Thus, his madhhab was ijtihad and the rejection of taqlid [and this is the position with all the scholars of past and present but not that of the common person or muqallid]. As a result of this he incurred great harm and was imprisoned with his Shaykh, Ibn Taymiyyah, in the same prison, though in isolation from him.

He was not released from the prison until after the death of the Shaykh. [The previous sentence may seem to indicate that they were imprisoned because of their not following a madhhab, yet their imprisonment had more to do with their 'aqidah, which was deemed to be deviant by the many powerful and ignorant scholars of the time, may Allâh have mercy upon them.]

He took to teaching and giving verdicts for a number of years and (all) the people without exception benefitted from him. The scholars also testified to his knowledge and piety. Ibn Hajar said about him, "He had a courageous heart, was vast in knowledge and was well acquainted with the differences (of opinion) and the madhahib of the Salaf." Shaykh ul-Islam, Muhammad ibn 'Ali ash-Shawkani said, "He restricted (himself) to the (most) authentic of evidences, and admired acting upon them. He did not depend upon opinion (ra'i), would overcome (others) with the truth and would not be harsh with anyone with respect to it."

Ibn Kathir said, "He was attached to occupying himself with knowledge, day and night. He would pray and recite the Qur'an much and was of excellent character, and showed great affection and friendship. He would not be jealous or envious." Ibn Kathir also said, "I do not know, in this time of ours, anyone in the world whose worship is greater than his. He used to have a particular manner with respect to the prayer. He would lengthen it a great deal, would extend its bowing and prostrating. Many of his associates would censure him at times but he would never return and leave alone this (action of his), may Allâh have mercy upon him."

Mulla 'Ali al-Qari said, "And whoever investigates the book Sharh Manazil as-Sa'irin (i.e., Madarij as-Salikin), it will become plain and clear to him that both of them (meaning Ibn Al-Qayyim and Ibn Taymiyyah) were amongst the most senior from Ahlus-Sunnah wal-Jama'ah and amongst the Awliya' (of Allâh) of this Ummah." Al-Hafidh As-Suyuti said, "And he became one of the senior scholars in exegesis (tafsir), hadith, 'usul, subsidiary matters (furu') and Arabic language."

He authored and compiled in the field of fiqh, 'usul, biography (siyar), history and the sciences of hadith. Alongsde this he was a linguist, well-acquainted with grammar. He also wrote much poetry.

He passed on to the mercy of His Lord at the latter time of Isha', on the night of Thursday, 13th of Rajab in the year 751H (1350CE) and was buried at the foot of Mount Qasiyun by Damascus, leaving behind many written works, amongst the most famous of which are:

Shifa' al-Alil

Miftah Dar as-Sa'adah

Za'ad al-Ma'ad fi Haydi Khayri'l-'Ibad

Hadiy al-Arwah ila Biladi'l-Afrah

Ighathatu'l-Lahfan fi Hukm Talaq al-Ghadban

Al-Jawab al-Kafi li man Sa'ala 'an Dawa' ash-Shafi'i

Madarij as-Salikin fi Manazil as-Sa'irin

Tahdhib Sunan Abi Dawud

As-Sawa'iq al-Mursalah 'alal-Jahmiyyah wa'l-Mu'attilah

Raf' Yadayn fi's-Salat

Kitab al-Kaba'ir

Hukm Tarik as-Salat

Al-Kalam at-Tayyib wal-'Amal as-Salih

Sharh Asma' al-Husna

A'lam al-Muqaqqi'in 'an Rabb al-'Alamin

May Allâh have mercy upon this great and noble Imam, benefit the world by him and elevate his position, rank after rank, in the Hereafter. Amin.

"A man said to one of the ascetics (those who devote themselves to Allah and have no interest in the world), amazed by his lack of interest in worldly matters: "I have never witnessed anyone who is more self-denying than you!" The man replied: "In fact, you are more self-denying than I. I have no interest in the world, which has neither permanence nor loyalty, while you are not interested in the Hereafter. So, which one of us is more self-denying?"

— Ibn Qayyim al-Jawziyya

Chapter One
A Genuine Sincerity

Having a genuine sincere niyya frees our intentions (niyya) from all impurities in order to come nearer to God (Allâh). Our niyya behind all prayers and acts of worship must always be obedience to Allâh and for the pleasure of Allâh. It is the continuous contemplation of our Creator, to the extent that one forgets the creation. Sincerity and honesty are always the conditions for Allâh's acceptance of good deeds performed in accordance with the teachings of the Messenger of Allâh (peace and blessings be upon him). Allâh has commanded us to worship Him alone, and to always be sincere towards Him in our religion (deen).

Abu Umama was a companion (sahabah) of Prophet Muhammad (peace and blessings be upon him). He said that a man once came to the Prophet (peace and blessings be upon him) and said: "If a man joined us in the fighting, but his niyya (intention) was just for fame and booty?" The Prophet (peace and blessings be upon him) said: "He would receive no reward from Allâh." The man did not like the Prophet's answer, so he repeated the question again and again. However, each time the Prophet (peace and blessings be upon him) said: "He would receive no reward from Allâh". Then the Prophet (peace and blessings be upon him) said: "Allâh only accepts actions that are intended purely for His pleasure." Abu Sa'id al-Khudri said that the Prophet (peace and blessings be upon him) told the Muslims in a Khutbah (prayer address) during the farewell pilgrimage: "Allâh will bless whoever hears my words and understands them, for it may be that those who pass on knowledge are not those who understands my words the best.

There are 4 important things about which the heart of a believer should feel no malice or any enmity: devoting one's actions always only to Allâh, being sincere and honest, being loyal, and giving advice to the Imams." What is meant here is that these 4 things will always strengthen the heart of the strong believer, and whoever distinguishes himself in them will have their heart purified from all matter of corruption, deceit, and evil. A true servant can only free himself from the shaytan (Iblis, the devil) only through strong sincere devotion. Allâh tells us in the Quran that Iblis (the devil) said to Him: *"Except those of Your servants who are sincere."*

It has been said that a very righteous man used to say: "O'Self! Be sincere and you will be pure always."' When any worldly things, in which the self finds comfort and in which the heart inclines, intrudes upon our prayer and worship, then it will harm the purity of our efforts and it will ruin our sincerity.

Any person that is preoccupied with life and their good fortune and is immersed deeply in their own desires and appetites, will get no reward from Allâh. For this reason it has been said that whoever can secure a true single moment of pure devotion to Allâh in this life will survive, for devotion is truly very rare and precious. Cleansing the heart of impurities is always challenging but necessary. Devotion is purifying the heart from impurities, whether a little or much, so that the intention of drawing nearer to Allâh is freed from all other motives, but that of only seeking Allâh's pleasure. This can only come from loving Allâh alone, who is so occupied and absorbed in contemplation of the next world (akhira), and so there remains in their heart no place for the love of this world.

Such a person must be devout and pure in all their ways and actions always, even when they eat, drink, and even when answering the calls of nature. With rare exceptions, anyone that is not like this in all their actions, will find the door of devotion closed in their life and face.

Therefore, the everyday actions of a person who is overwhelmed by their love for Allâh and the next life (akhira, life after death) only, are characterized by this love and they are, in fact, pure devotion. In the same way, anyone who is overwhelmed by their love and preoccupation with this life, or by authority or status, will be so overwhelmed by such things that no act of worship of any kind, be it fasting or prayer, would be acceptable.

The cure for loving this world so much is to break the desires of the self, and to end the greed and love for this world, and to purify the self and to prepare it for the next world. This will then become the state of their heart and so sincere devotion will become much easier to attain. There are a great many actions where a person acts, thinking that they are purely intended for Allâh's pleasure, but this person is deluded and fails to see the defects in them.

It has been said that a man was used to love praying in the first row in the Masjid (mosque). One day he overslept and was late for the prayer, so he prayed in the second row. And he felt embarrassment when the people saw him in the second row, he then realized that the pleasure and satisfaction of the heart that he used to feel from praying in the first row were only due to him seeing people seeing him in the first row and admiring him for it. This is a subtle and intangible condition and actions are rarely safe from it.

Apart from those whom Allâh has assisted, few are aware of such delicate and small matters. Those who do not realize it fast, only come to see their good deeds appearing as bad ones on the Day of Resurrection. They are the ones referred to in Allâh's words, And something will come to them from Allâh which they had never anticipated, for the evil of their deeds will become very clear to them.

"Shall We tell you who lost most in respect of their deeds? Those whose efforts were astray in the life of this world, while they thought that they were doing good deeds." Yaqub (peace and blessings be upon him) said: *"A devout person is someone who always conceals the things that are good, in the same way that they conceal the things that are bad."*

As-Sousi once said: "True devotion is to lose the faculty of being conscious of your devotion; for someone who identifies devotion in his devotion is a person whose devotion is in need of devotion." To contemplate devotion is to admire it, and admiration is an illness, an affliction; and that which is pure is whatever is free of all afflictions. This means that one's deeds must be purified from any self-admiration concerning the actions they entail.

Ayyub (peace and blessings be upon him) said: "It is much harder for the people of action to purify their intentions than it is to execute any of their actions."

Some people have also said: "To be devout for a short while is truly to survive forever, but devotion is very rare."

The most difficult thing for the self is "*devotio*n," when the self does not have the good fortune of being endowed with it. Forsaking action for the sake of other people is to seek their admiration. Be very careful! Because to act for the sake of their admiration is to associate others with Allâh. Devotion is when Allâh loves you and frees you from all such states.

"Abd al-Rahman bin 'Awf said: "We were put to trial with adversity and we were able to sustain it, but when we were tried with prosperity we failed to show patience."

— Ibn Qayyim al-Jawziyya

Chapter Two
THE NATURE OF OUR INTENTION

The intention (niyya) of a person is not their utterance of the words: "I intend to do so and so." It must be from the heart which runs like conquests inspired by Allâh. At times it is made easy, at other times, it is difficult. A person whose heart is overwhelmingly righteous finds it easy to summon good intentions often. Such a person has a heart generally inclined to the roots of goodness which, most of the time, blossom into the manifestation of good deeds and actions. As for those whose hearts incline towards and are overwhelmed by worldly matters, they find this very difficult to accomplish and even obligatory acts of worship may become very difficult and tiresome.

The Prophet: said: "Actions are only by intention, and every man shall only have what he intended. Thus he or she whose hijra was for Allâh and His Messenger, then their hijra was for Allâh and His Messenger, but a person whose hijra was to achieve some worldly benefit or to take some woman or man in marriage, then their hijra was for that for which he made hijra."

Imam ash-Shafi'i said: "This hadith is a third of all knowledge." The words, "actions are only by intention (niyya)", meaning that deeds which are performed in accordance with the Sunnah are only acceptable and rewarded if the intentions behind them were sincere. It is like the saying of the Prophet, may Allâh bless him and grant him peace, actions depend upon their outcome.

Likewise, the words, "every man shall only have what he intended", mean that the reward for an action depends upon the intention behind it. After stating this principle, the Prophet: gave examples of it by saying, "Thus he whose hijra was for Allâh and His Messenger, his hijra was for Allâh and His Messenger, and he whose hijra was to achieve some worldly benefit or to take some woman in marriage, his hijra was for that for which he made hijra." So deeds which are apparently identical may differ, because the intentions behind them are different in degrees of goodness and badness, from one person to another.

Good intentions do not change the nature of forbidden actions. The ignorant should not misconstrue the meaning of the hadth and think that good intentions could turn for- bidden actions into acceptable ones. The above saying of the Prophet: specifically relates to acts of worship and permissible actions, not to forbidden ones. Worship and permissible actions can be turned into forbidden ones because of the intentions behind them, and permissible actions can become either good or bad deeds by intention; but wrong actions cannot become acts of worship, even with good intentions.' When bad intentions are accompanied by flaws in the actions themselves, then their gravity and punishment are multiplied.

Any praiseworthy act must be rooted in sound intentions; only then should it be deemed worthy of reward. The fundamental principle should be that the act is intended for the worship of Allâh alone. If our intention is.to show off, then these same acts of worship will in fact be- come acts of disobedience. As for permissible deeds, they all involve intentions which can potentially turn them into excellent acts which bring a man nearer to Allâh and confer on him the gift of closeness to Him.

Excellence of Intention

Omar Ibn al-Khuttab, may Allâh be pleased with him, said: "The best acts are doing what Allâh has commanded, to stay far away from what Allâh has forbidden. And having honest and sincere intentions towards whatever Allâh has required of us."

Some of our predecessors said: "Many small actions are made greater by our intentions behind them. Many great actions, on the other hand, are made smaller because the intentions behind them are lacking, meaning you did not intend to do them."

Yahya Ibn Abu Kathir said: "Try to learn about intentions, for their importance is greater than the importance of actions."

Ibn Omar once heard a man who was putting on his Al-hiram say: "O Allâh! I intend to do the Hajj and Umrah." So he said to him: "Is it not in fact the people whom you are telling of your intentions, because Allâh already knows what is in your heart?" The good intentions are exclusively the concern of the heart, so they should not be voiced during worship.

Excellence of Knowledge and Teaching

There are many proofs in the Quran concerning the excellence of knowledge and the transmission of it. Allâh, the Glorious, says: Allâh will raise up to higher ranks those of you who believe and those who have been given knowledge. And those who know equal to those who do not know.

Also, in the hadith, the Prophet, peace and blessings be upon him: says, "When Allâh wants good for someone, He gives them understanding of the deen." He also said, "Allâh makes the way to the Beautiful Garden easy for those that tread a path in search of knowledge."

Travelling on the path to knowledge is both to walking along an actual pathway, such as walking to the assemblies of the ulama', as well as to following a metaphysical path, such as studying and memorizing. This means that Allâh makes learning the useful knowledge that is sought and makes it easier for the seeker, clearing the way for him and smoothing their journey. Some of our predecessors used to say: "Is there anyone seeking knowledge, so that we can assist them in finding it."

This hadith also alludes to the road leading to the Beautiful Garden on the Day of Judgment, which is the straight path, and to what precedes it and what comes after it. Knowledge is the shortest path to Allâh and His love. Whoever travels the road of knowledge reaches Allâh and the Garden by the shortest route. Knowledge also clears our way out of darkness, such as ignorance, doubt and skepticism. It is why Allâh called His beautiful Book, "Light".

Al-Bukhari and Muslim have reported on the authority of Abdullah Ibn Omar that the Messenger of Allâh, said: "Truly, Allâh will not take away knowledge by snatching it away, but He will take it away by taking the lives of the people of knowledge one by one until none of them are alive. Then the people will adopt ignorant people as their leaders. They will be asked to deliver judgments and they will give answers without knowledge, so they will go astray and lead others astray."

When 'Ubadah Ibn as-Samit was asked about this hadith he said: "If you want, I will tell you what the highest knowledge is that raises people in rank: it is humility." He said there are two types of knowledge. The first produces its fruit in the heart. It is knowledge of Allâh, His Names, His Attributes, and His Acts that commands fear, respect, exaltation, love, supplication and reliance on Him. This is the beneficial type of knowledge. As Ibn Masud said: "They will recite the Quran, but it will not go beyond their throats. The Quran is only beneficial when it reaches our heart and is firmly planted in it."

Al-Hasan said: "There are two kinds of knowledge: the knowledge of the tongue, which can be a case against the son of Adam, as is mentioned in the hadith of the Prophet, peace and blessings be upon him: 'The Quran is either a case for you or a case against you"; and knowledge of the heart, which is beneficial knowledge. The second kind is the beneficial kind which raises people to higher ranks; it is the inner knowledge which is absorbed by the heart and puts it right. The knowledge that is on the tongue is taken lightly by people: neither those who possess it, nor anyone else, act upon it, nor then it vanishes when their owners vanish on the Day of Judgment, when creation will be brought to account."

Prophet Mohamad, may Allâh bless him and grant him peace, said, "You will receive the reward for sadaqa even when you have sexual intercourse with your wife." The sahaba said, "Will we truly be rewarded for satisfying our physical desires?" He replied, "If you have haram intercourse (an adulterous affair), then you will be committing a sin, but if you have halal intercourse with your wife, you will be rewarded." Imam an-Nawawi said, "This hadith clearly shows that permissible actions become acts of obedience if there is a good intention behind them; sexual intercourse becomes an act of worship if it is accompanied by any one of the following good intentions: keeping company with your wife in kindness; hoping to have good and righteous offspring; guarding your chastity and also that of your wife; controlling haram lustful glances or thoughts, or haram intercourse; and any other good intention."

"It shows that being steadfast and avoiding sins, which are connected with the tongue and sexual organ, are the most difficult type of endurance, since their motives are very powerful and the acts are easy to commit."

— Ibn Qayyim al-Jawziyya

Chapter Three
TYPES OF HEART

Just as the heart may be described in terms of being alive or dead, the heart may also be regarded as belonging to one of three types; these are the healthy heart, the sick heart, and the dead heart.

The Healthy Heart

On the Day of Resurrection, only those who come to Allâh with a healthy heart will be saved. Allâh says: The day on which neither wealth nor sons will be of any use, except for whoever has a good heart.

The healthy heart is a heart cleansed from any passion that challenges what Allâh commands, or disputes what Allâh forbids. It is free from any impulses which contradict His good. As a result, it is safeguarded against the worship of anything other than Allâh, and seeks the judgment of no other except that of His Messenger: Its services are exclusively reserved for Allâh only, willingly and lovingly, with total reliance, relating all matters to Him, in fear, hope and sincere dedication.

When the heart loves, its love is in the way of Allâh. If it detests, it detests in the light of what Allâh detests. When it gives, it gives for Allâh. Nevertheless, all this will not suffice for its salvation until it is free from following, or taking as its guide, anyone other than His Messenger, peace and blessings be upon him."

A servant with a healthy heart must dedicate it to its journey's end and not base his actions and speech on those of any other person except Allâh's Messenger, peace and blessings be upon him. He must not give precedence to any other faith or words or deeds over those of Allâh and His Messenger, may Allâh bless him and grant him peace.

Allâh says: Oh you who believe, do not put yourselves above Allâh and His Messenger, but fear Allâh, for Allâh is Hearing and Knowing.

The Dead Heart

The dead heart is the opposite of the healthy heart. It does not know its Lord and does not worship Him as He commands, in the way which He likes, and with which He is pleased. It clings instead to lusts and desires, even if these are likely to incur Allâh's wrath and displeasure. It worships things other than Allâh, and its loves and its hatreds, and its giving and its withholding, arise from its whims, which are of paramount importance to it and preferred above the pleasure of Allâh. Its whims are its Imam. Its lust is its guide. Its ignorance is its leader. Its crude impulses are its impetus. It is immersed in its concern with worldly objectives. It is drunk with its own fancies and its love for hasty, fleeting pleasures. It is called to Allâh and the akhira from a distance but it does not respond to any advice. Instead it follows any scheming, cunning shaytan. Life angers and pleases it. And Passion makes it deaf and blind to anything except what is evil.

To associate and keep company with the owner of such a heart is to tempt illness. Living with him is as taking poison, and befriending him means utter destruction.

The Sick Heart

This is a heart with life in it, as well as illness. The former sustains it at one moment, the latter at another, and it follows whichever one of the two manages to dominate it. It has love for Allâh, faith in Him, sincerity towards Him, and reliance upon Him, and these are what give it life. But also it has a craving for lust and pleasure. It prefers them, and strives to experience them. It is full of self-admiration, which can lead to its own destruction. It listens to two callers: one calling it to Allâh and His Prophet, and the akhira; and the other calling it to the fleeting pleasures of this world. So it responds to whichever one of the two happens to have most influence over it at the time.

The first heart is alive and healthy, submitted to Allâh, sensitive and aware; the second is brittle, dead; the third wavers between either its safety or its ruin.

"There are four agents that induce people to commit prohibited acts: the soul of the man, the devil assigned to him, his desire, and this world. In order to keep away from prohibited matters a man has to fight and resist all these. Needless to say, it is the most difficult and strenuous thing for the soul."

— Ibn Qayyim al-Jawziyya

Chapter Four

SYMPTOMS OF THE HEART'S SICKNESS AND SIGNS OF ITS HEALTH

The Signs of a Sick Heart

A servant's heart may be ill, and seriously deteriorating, while he remains oblivious of its condition. It may even die without him realizing it. The symptoms of its sickness, or the signs of its death, are that its owner is not aware of the harm that results from the damage caused by wrong actions, and is unperturbed by his ignorance of the truth or by his false beliefs. Since the living heart experiences pain as a result of any ugliness that t encounters and through its recognizing its ignorance of the truth (to a degree that corresponds to its level of awareness), it is capable of recognizing the onset of decay and the increase in the severity of the remedy that will be needed to stop it, but then sometimes it prefers to put up with the pain rather than undergo the arduous trial of the cure'

Some of the many signs of the heart's sickness is its turning away from good foods to harmful ones, from good remedies to shameful sickness. The healthy heart prefers what is beneficial and healing to what is harmful and damaging; the sick heart prefers the opposite. The most beneficial sustenance for the heart is faith and the best medicine is the Quran.

The Signs of a Healthy Heart

For the heart to be healthy it should depart from this life and arrive in the next, and then settle there as if it were one of its people; it only carne to this life as a passer-by, taking whatever provisions it needed and then returning home. As the Prophet, may Allâh bless him and grant him peace, said to Abdullah Ibn Urnar, "Be in this world as if you were a stranger or a passer-by.'" The more diseased the heart is, the more it desires this world; it dwells in it until it becomes like one of its own people. This healthy heart continues to trouble its owner until he returns to Allâh, and is at peace with Him, and joins Him, like a lover driven by compulsion who finally reaches his beloved. Besides his love for Him he needs no other, and after invoking Him no other invocations are needed. Serving Him precludes the need to serve any other.

If this heart misses its share of reciting the Quran and invoking Allâh, or completing one of the prescribed acts of worship, then its owner suffers more distress than a cautious man who suffers because of the loss of money or a missed opportunity to make it. It longs to serve, just as a famished person longs for food and drink.

Yahya Ibn Mu'adh said: "Whoever is pleased with serving Allâh, everything will be pleased to serve him; and whoever finds pleasure in contemplating Allâh, all the people will find pleasure in contemplating him."

This heart has only one concern: that all its actions, and its inner thoughts and utterances, are obedient to Allâh. It is more careful with its time than the meanest people are with their money, so that it will not be spent wastefully. When it enters into the prayer, all its worldly worries and anxieties vanish and it finds its comfort and bliss in adoring its Lord.

It does not cease to mention Allâh, nor does tire of serving Him, and it find intimate company with no-one save a person who guides it to Allâh and reminds it of Him.

Its attention to the correctness of its action is greater than its attention to the action itself. It is scrupulous in making sure that the intentions behind its actions are sincere and pure and that they result in good deeds.

As well as and in spite of all this, it not only testifies to the generosity of Allâh in giving it the opportunity to carry out such actions, but also testifies to its own imperfection and shortcomings in executing them.

The Causes of Sickness of the Heart

The temptations to which the heart is exposed are what cause its sickness. These are the temptations of desires and fancies. The former cause intentions and the will to be corrupted, and the latter cause knowledge and belief to falter.

Hudhayfa Ibn al-Yamani, may Allâh be pleased with him, said: "The Messenger of Allâh said, 'Temptations are presented to the heart, one by one. Any heart that accepts them will be left with a black stain, but any heart that rejects them will be left with a mark of purity, so that hearts are of two types: a dark heart that has turned away and become like an overturned vessel, and a pure heart that will never be harmed by temptation for as long as the earth and the heavens exist. The dark heart only recognizes good and denounces evil when this suits its desires and whims.'" He, may Allâh bless him and grant him peace, placed hearts, when exposed to temptation, into two categories:

First, a heart which, when II is exposed to temptation, absorbs it like a sponge that soaks up water, leaving a black stain in it. It continues to absorb each temptation that is offered to it until it is darkened and corrupted, which is what he meant by "like an overturned vessel". When this happens, two dangerous sicknesses take hold of it and plunge it into rum: The first is that of its confusing good with evil, to such an extent that it does not recognize the former and does not denounce the latter. This sickness may even gain hold of it to such an extent that it believes good to be evil and vice-versa, the Sunnah to be bida' and vice-versa, the truth to be false and falsity to be the truth.

The second is that of its setting up its desires as its judge, over and above what the Prophet taught, so that it is enslaved and led by its whims and fancies. Second, a pure heart in which the light of faith is bright and from which its radiance shines. When temptation is presented to pure hearts such as this, they oppose it and reject it, and so their light and illumination only increase.

"Realization of the divine decree, and remembering that the person who caused you pain was unjust, but the One who decreed it for you and executed it at the hand of this unjust person, was not unjust."

— Ibn Qayyim al-Jawziyya

Chapter Five
THE FOUR POISONS OF THE HEART

You should know that all acts of disobedience are poison to the heart and cause its sickness and ruin. They result in its will running off course, against that of Allâh, and so its sickness festers and increases. Ibn al-Mubarak said: I have seen wrong actions killing hearts, and their degradation may lead to their becoming addicted to them. Turning away from wrong actions gives life to the hearts, and opposing your self is best for it.

Whoever is concerned with the health and life of his heart, must rid it of the effects of such poisons, and then protect it by avoiding new ones. If he takes any by mistake, then he should hasten to wipe out their effect by turning in repentance and seeking forgiveness from Allâh, as well as by doing good deeds that will wipe out his wrong actions.

By the four poisons we mean unnecessary talking, unrestrained glances, too much food and keeping bad company. Of all the poisons, these are the most widespread and have the greatest effect on a heart's well-being.

Unnecessary Talking

It is reported in al-Musnad, on the authority of Anas, that the Prophet said: "The faith of a servant is not put right until his heart is put right, and his heart is not put right until his tongue is put right.'" This shows that the Prophet has made the purification of faith conditional on the purification of the heart, and the purification of the heart conditional on the purification of the tongue.

At-Tirmidhi relates in a hadith on the authority of Ibn Omar: "Do not talk excessively without remembering Allâh, because such excessive talk without the mention of Allâh causes the heart to harden, and the person furthest from Allâh is a person with a hard heart."

Omar Ibn al-Khuttab, may Allâh be pleased with him, said: "A person who talks too much is a person who often makes mistakes, and someone who often makes mistakes, often has wrong actions. The Fire has a priority over such a frequent sinner."

In a hadith related on the authority of Mu'adh, the Prophet said, "Shall not tell you how to control all that?" I said, "Yes do, Messenger of Allâh." So he held his tongue between his fingers, and then he said: "Restrain this." Said, "Prophet of Allâh, are we accountable for what we say?" He said, "May your mother be bereft by your loss! Is there anything more than the harvest of the tongues that throws people on their faces (or he said 'on their noses') into the Fire?"

What is meant here by 'the harvest of the tongues' is the punishment for saying forbidden things. A man, through his actions and words, sows the seeds of either good or evil. On the Day of Resurrection he harvests their fruits. Those who sow the seeds of good words and deeds harvest honor and blessings; those who sow the seeds of evil words and deeds reap only regret and remorse.

A hadith related by Abu Huraira says, "What mostly causes people to be sent to the Fire are the two openings: the mouth and the private parts."

Abu Huraira also related that the Messenger of Allâh: said, "The servant speaks words, the consequences of which he does not realize, and for which he is sent down into the depths of the Fire further than the distance between the east and the west.'"

The same hadith was transmitted by at-Tirmidhi with slight variations: "The servant says something that he thinks is harmless, and or which he will be plunged into the depths of the Fire as far as seventy autumns."

Uqba Ibn Amir said: "I said: 'O Messenger of Allâh, what is our best way of surviving?' He, may Allâh bless him and grant him peace, replied: 'Guard your tongue, make your house suffice for sheltering your privacy, and weep for your wrong actions.'" '

It has been related on the authority of Sahl Ibn Sa'd that the Prophet said, "Whoever can guarantee what is between his jaws and what is between his legs, I guarantee him the Garden."

It has also been related by Abu Huraira, may Allâh be pleased with him, that the Prophet, may Allâh bless him and grant him peace, said, "Let whoever believes in Allâh and the Last Day either speak good or remain silent."

Thus talking can either be good, in which case it is com- mendable, or bad, in which case it is haram. The Prophet said: "Everything the children of Adam say goes against them, except for their enjoining good and forbidding evil, and remembering Allâh, Glorious and Mighty is He." This was reported by at-Tirmidhi and Ibn Ma'jah on the authority of Umm Habiba, may Allâh be pleased with her.

Omar Ibn al-Khuttab visited Abu Bakr, may Allâh be pleased with them, and found him pulling his tongue with his fingers. Omar said "Stop' may Allâh forgive you'" Abu Bakr replied: "This tongue has brought me to dangerous places."

Abdullah Ibn Mas'ud said: "By Allâh, besides Whom no god exists, nothing deserves a long prison sentence more than my tongue." He also used to say: "Tongue, say good and you will profit; desist from saying evil things and you will be safe; otherwise you will find only regret."

Abu Huraira reported that Ibn al-Abbas said: "A person will not feel greater fury or anger for any part of his body on the Day of judgment more than what he will feel for his tongue, unless he only used it for saying or enjoining good."

Al-Hassan said: "Whoever does not hold his tongue cannot understand his deen."

The least harmful of a tongue's faults is talking about whatever does not concern it. The following hadith of the Prophet is enough to indicate the harm of this fault: "One of the merits of a person's Islam is his abandoning what does not concern him."

Abu Ubaida related that al-Hassan said: "One of the signs of Allâh's abandoning a servant is His making him preoccupied with what does not concern him."

Sahl said, "Whoever talks about what does not concern him is deprived of truthfulness." As we have already mentioned above, this is the least harmful of the tongue's faults. There are far worse things, like backbiting, gossiping, obscene and misleading talk, two-faced and hypocritical talk, showing off, quarrelling, bickering, singing, lying, mockery, derision and falsehood; and there are many more faults which can affect a servant's tongue, ruining his heart and causing him to lose both his happiness and pleasure in this life, and his success and profit in the next life. Allâh is the One to Whom we turn for assistance.

Unrestrained Glances

The unrestrained glance results in the one who looks becoming attracted to what he sees, and in the imprinting of an image of what he sees in his heart. This can result in several kinds of corruption in the heart of the servant. The following are a number of them: It has been related that the Prophet once said words to the effect: "The glance is a poisoned arrow of shaytan. Whoever lowers his gaze for Allâh, He will bestow upon him a refreshing sweetness which he will find in his heart on the day that he meets Him."

Shaytan enters with the glance, for he travels with it, faster than the wind blowing through an empty place. He makes what is seen appear more beautiful than it really is, and transforms it into an idol for the heart to worship. Then he promises it false rewards, lights the fire of desires within it, and fuels it with the wood of forbidden actions, which the servant would not have committed had it not been for this distorted image.

This distracts the heart and makes it forget the more important concerns. It stands between it and them; and so the heart loses its straight path and falls into the pit of desire and ignorance. Allâh, Mighty and Glorious is He, says: And do not obey anyone whose heart We have made forgetful in remembering us who follows his own desires, and whose affair has exceeded all bounds.

The unrestrained gaze causes all three afflictions. It has been said that between the eye and the heart is an immediate connection; if the eyes are corrupted, then the heart follows. It becomes like a rubbish heap where all the dirt and filth and rottenness collect, and so there is no room for love for Allâh, relating all matters to Him, aware- ness of being in His presence, and feeling joy at His proximity only the opposite of these things can inhabit such a heart. Staring and gazing without restraint is disobedience to Allâh: Tell the believing men to lower their gaze and guard their modesty; that is more purifying for them. Surely Allâh is aware of what they do.

Only the one who obeys Allâh's commands is content in this world, and only the servant who obeys Allâh will survive in the next world. Furthermore, letting the gaze roam free cloaks the heart with darkness, just as lowering the gaze for Allâh clothes it in light. After the above ayah, Allâh, the Glorious and Mighty, says in the same surah of the Quran: Allâh is the light of the heavens and the earth: the likeness of His light is as if there were a niche, and in the niche is a lamp, and in the lamp is a glass, and the glass as it were a brilliant star, lit from a blessed tree, an olive, neither of the east nor of the west, whose oil is well high luminous, though fire scarce touched it. Light upon light. Allâh guides whomever He wants to His Light. Allâh strikes metaphors for man; and Allâh knows all things.

When the heart is a light, countless good comes to it from all directions. If it is dark, then clouds of evil and afflictions come from all directions to cover it up.

Letting the gaze run loose also makes the heart blind to distinguishing between truth and falsehood, between the Sunnah and innovation; while lowering it for Allâh, the Mighty and Exalted, gives it a penetrating, true and distinguishing insight.

A righteous man once said: "Whoever enriches his outward behavior by following the Sunnah, and makes his inward soul wealthy through contemplation, and averts his gaze away from looking at what is forbidden, and avoids anything of a doubtful nature, and feeds solely on what is halal his inner sight will never falter."

Rewards for actions come in kind. Whoever lowers his gaze from what Allâh has forbidden, Allâh will give his inner sight abundant light.

Too Much Food

The consumption of small amounts of food guarantees tenderness of the heart, strength of the intellect, humility of the self, weakness of desires, and gentleness of temperament. Immoderate eating brings about the opposite of these praiseworthy qualities.

Al-Miqdam Ibn Ma'd Yakrib said: "I heard the Messenger of Allâh say: 'The son of Adam fills no vessel more displeasing to Allâh than his stomach. A few morsels should be enough for him to preserve his strength.

If he must fill it, then he should allow a third for his food, a third for his drink and leave a third empty for easy breathing.'"

Excessive eating induces many kinds of harm. It makes the body incline towards disobedience to Allâh and makes worship and obedience seem laborious such evils are bad enough in themselves. A full stomach and excessive eating have caused many a wrong action and inhibited much worship. Whoever safeguards against the evils of overfilling his stomach has prevented great evil. It is easier for shaytan to control a person who has filled his stomach with food and drink, which is why it has often been said: "Restrict the pathways of shaytan by fasting."

It has been reported that when a group of young men from the Tribe of Israel were worshipping, and it was time for them to break their fast, a man stood up and said: "Do not eat too much, otherwise you will drink too much, and then you will end up sleeping too much, and then you will lose too much."

The Prophet and his companions, may Allâh be pleased with them, used to go hungry quite frequently. Al- though this was often due to a shortage of food, Allâh de- creed the best and most favorable conditions for His Messenger, may Allâh bless him and grant him peace. This is why Ibn Omar and his father before him in spite of the abundance of food available to them modelled their eating habits on those of the Prophet. It has been reported that Aisha, may Allâh be pleased with her, said: "From the time of their arrival in Madina up until his death. The family of Mohamad never ate their fill of bread made from wheat three nights in a row."

Ibrahim Ibn Adham said: "Anyone who controls his stomach is in control of his deen, and anyone who controls his hunger is in control of good behavior. Disobedience towards Allâh is nearest to a person who is satiated with a full stomach, and furthest away from a person who is hungry."

Keeping Bad Company

Unnecessary companionship is a chronic disease that causes much harm. How often have the wrong kind of companionship and intermixing deprived people of Allâh's generosity, planting discord m their hearts which even the passage of time even if it were long enough for mountains to be won away has been unable to dispel. In keeping such company one can find the roots of loss, both in this life and in the next life.

A servant should benefit from companionship. In order to do so he should divide people into four categories, and be careful not to get them mixed up, for once one of them is mixed with another, then evil can find its way through to him: The first category are those people whose company is like food: it is indispensable, night or day. Once a servant has taken his need from it, he leaves it be until he requires it again, and so on. These are the people with knowledge of Allâh of His commands, of the scheming of His enemies, and of the diseases of the heart and their remedies- who wish well for Allâh, His Prophet and His servants. Associating with this type of person is an achievement in itself.

The second category are those people whose company is like a medicine. They are only required when a disease sets in. When you are healthy, you have no need of them. However, mixing with them is sometimes necessary for your live hood, businesses, consultation and the like. Once what you need from them has been fulfilled, mixing with them should be avoided.

The third category are those people whose company is harmful. Mixing with this type of person is like a disease, in all its variety and degrees and strengths and weaknesses. Associating with one or some of them is like an incurable chronic disease. You will never profit either in this life or in the next life if you have them for company, and you will surely lose either one or both of your deen and your livelihood because of them. If their companionship has taken hold of you and is established, then it becomes a fatal, terrifying sickness.

Amongst such people are those who neither speak any good that might benefit you, nor listen closely to you so that they might benefit from you. They do not know their souls and consequently put their selves in their rightful place. When they speak, their words fall on their listeners' hearts like the lashes of a cane, while all the while they are lull of admiration for and delight in their own words.

They cause distress to those in their company, while believing that they are the sweet scent of the gathering. If they are silent, they are heavier than a massive millstone, too heavy to carry or even drag across the floor.

All in all, mixing with anyone who is bad for the soul will not last, even if it is unavoidable. It can be one of the most distressing aspects of a servant's life that he is plagued by such person, with whom it may be necessary to associate. In such a relationship, a servant should cling to good behavior, only presenting him with his outward appearance, while disguising his inner soul, until Allâh offers him a way out of his affliction and the means of escape from this situation.

The fourth category are those people whose company is doom itself. It is like taking poison: its victim either finds an antidote or perishes. Many people belong to this category. They are the people of religious innovation and misguidance, those who abandon the Sunnah of the Messenger of Allâh and advocate other beliefs. They call what is the Sunnah a bid'a and vice-versa. A man with any intellect should not sit in their assemblies nor mix with them. The result of doing so will either be the death of his heart or, at the very best, falling seriously ill.

What Gives the Heart Life and Sustenance?

You should know that acts of obedience are essential to the wellbeing of the servant's heart, just in the same way that food and drink are to that of the body. All wrong actions are the same as poisonous foods, and they inevitably harm the heart. The servant feels the need to worship his Lord, Mighty and Glorious Is He, for he is naturally in constant need of His help and assistance.

In order to maintain the wellbeing of his body, the servant carefully follows a strict diet. He habitually and constantly eats good food at regular intervals, and is quick to free his stomach of harmful elements if he happens to eat bad food by mistake.

The wellbeing of the servant's heart, however, is far more important than that of his body, for while the wellbeing of his body enables him to lead a life that is free from illnesses in this world, that of the heart ensures him both a fortunate life in this world and eternal bliss in the next.

In the same way, while the death of the body cuts the servant off from this world, the death of the heart results in everlasting anguish. A righteous man once said, "How odd, that some people mourn for the one whose body has died, but never mourn for the one whose heart has died and yet the death of the heart is far more serious!"

Thus acts of obedience are indispensable to the wellbeing of the heart. It is worthwhile mentioning the following acts of obedience here, since they are very necessary and essential for the servant's heart: Dhikr of Allâh ta'Aia, recitation of the Noble Quran, seeking Allâh's forgiveness, making du as invoking Allâh's blessings and peace on the Prophet, may Allâh bless him and grant him peace, and praying at night.

"The point is that the degree of hardship when exercising patience from committing sins depends on the strength or weakness of the motives for that sin."

— Ibn Qayyim al-Jawziyya

Chapter Six

REMEMBRANCE OF ALLÂH AND RECITATION OF THE QURAN

Ibn Taimiyya wrote, "Remembrance of Allâh is to the heart what water is to fish. What happens to a fish when it is taken out of water?" Imam Shams ad-Din Ibn al-Qayyim wrote about nearly eighty benefits that come with dhikru 'llah in his book al-Wabil al-Sayyib. We shall quote some of them here, although we recommend the reader to refer to this book itself because of its great value.

Remembrance of Allâh is sustenance for both the heart and the spirit. If the servant is deprived of it he becomes like a body which has been deprived of food.

Remembrance of Allâh also drives away shaytan, suppressing him and breaking him; it is pleasing to the Merciful, Mighty and Exalted is He, dispels worry and melancholy from the heart, adorns it with delight and joy, fills the heart and face with light, and cloaks the one who re- members Allâh with dignity, gentleness and freshness. It instils love for Allâh, fear of Him, and relating all matters to Him. It also enhances Allâh's remembrance of His servant, for as Allâh says: So remember Me, I will remember you.

Even if this were the only reward for the remembrance of Allâh, it would be mercy and honor enough, for such a heart IS always aware and free from wrong actions. Although remembrance is one of the easiest forms of worship, the mercy and honor that it brings cannot be achieved by any other means. Abu Huraira reported that the Prophet said, "Whoever recites the words, 'There is no god but Allâh, the One, having no partner with Him. Sovereignty belongs to Him and All praise is due to Him, and He is Powerful over everything', one hundred times every day, there is a reward equal to freeing ten slaves for him, and a hundred good actions are recorded for him, and a hundred wrong actions are removed from his record. That is a safeguard for him against shaytan on that day until evening, and no one brings anything more excellent than this, except the one who has done more than this (that is, who recites these words more than one hundred times)."

Jabir reported that the Prophet said, "Whoever recites the words, 'Glory be to Allâh and His is the praise', will have a palm tree planted for him in the Garden."

Ibn Mas'ud, may Allâh be pleased with him, said, "To Praise Allâh, may He be Exalted, is more dear to me than spending the same number of dinars (as the number of times I praise Him) in the way of Allâh."

Remembrance of Allâh is a remedy for hard hearts. A man once told al-Hassan, "Abu Sa'id, I complain to you about the hardness of my heart." He said, "Soften it with the remembrance of Allâh." Makhul said, "Remembrance of Allâh is (a sign of) health, while remembrance of people is like a disease."

A man once asked Salman, "Which deeds are the best?" He said, "Haven't you read in the Quran: And the remembrance of Allâh is greatest."

Abu Musa once related that the Prophet said, "The difference between the one who remembers his Lord and the one who does not is like the difference between the living and the dead."

Abdullah Ibn Busr related that a man once told the Prophet, "The roads to good are many and I am unable to take all of them, so please tell me something to which I can hold fast, but do not overburden me lest I forget it." He said, "Make sure that your tongue is moist and supple with the remembrance of Allâh, the Exalted."

Continual remembrance of Allâh increases a servant's good witnesses on the Day of Resurrection. It is a means which prevents him from talking in the wrong way, such as backbiting and spreading tales and their like. Either the tongue is mentioning Allâh and remembering Him, or it is talking incorrectly.

Whoever has the gates of remembrance opened to him has an opening to his Lord, Mighty and Glorious is He, through which he will find what he seeks. If he finds Allâh, he has found everything. If he misses the opportunity, he has missed everything.

There are several types of remembrance. The remembrance of the Names of Allâh, Mighty and Glorious is He, the remembrance of His Attributes, and praising Him and thanking Him. All of these can take the form of saying, for example, 'Glory be to Allâh', 'Praise be to Allâh', 'there is no god but Allâh'. A servant can also remember Allâh by referring to His Names and Attributes, such as by saying, for example, "Allâh, Mighty and Glorious is He, Hears all that his servants say and do"; or by mentioning what He has commanded and what He has forbidden, such as saying, "Allâh, the Mighty and Glorious, commands such and such, or forbids such and such".

A servant can also remember Allâh by talking about His blessings, while the best type of remembrance is the recitation of the Quran, because this contains remedies to cure the heart from all illnesses. Allâh, the Exalted, says: Mankind! There has come to you a protection from your Lord and a healing for what is in your hearts, and for those who believe, a guidance and a mercy.

And also:

We send down in the Quran that which is a healing and a mercy for those who believe. All the illnesses of the heart result from desires and doubt, and the Quran is a cure for both. It has enough clear signs and proofs to distinguish between truth and falsehood, and thus it cures the diseases of doubt which ruin knowledge, understanding and perception, by enabling a person to see things as they really are.

Whoever studies the Quran, and allows it to be absorbed by his heart, will recognize truth and falsehood and will be able to distinguish between them, just as he is able to distinguish between night and day.

As for curing the diseases that arise from desires, it is because it contains wisdom and good counsel. This recommends avoiding worldly gains and inspires a yearning for the akhira.

The Prophet once said, "Whoever wants to love Allâh and His Messenger should read the Quran."

The Quran is also the best means for bringing the servant nearer to his Lord, Glorious and Exalted is He. Khabbab Ibn al-Arat said to a man, "Draw closer to Allâh as much as you can, and remember that you can do so by no means more pleasing to Him than using His own words."

Ibn Mas'ud said, "Whoever loves the Quran loves Allâh and His Messenger," and Sayyedi Uthman Ibn Affan, may Allâh be pleased with him, sad, "If your hearts were really pure, they would never have enough of reciting Allâh's words." All in all, the most beneficial thing for the servant is to remember Allâh, Mighty and Glorious is He, constantly: Surely in the remembrance of Allâh do hearts find rest. The best kind of remembrance is to recite the Book of Allâh, the Glorious and Exalted.

"Allah has made patience the means for attaining His love, His companionship, His help and support, and His good rewards. This is sufficient honour and blessings."

— Ibn Qayyim al-Jawziyya

Chapter Seven

SEEKING ALLÂH'S FORGIVENESS

Forgiveness is being shielded from the harmful consequences of wrong actions, and the veiling of them. Seeking forgiveness is mentioned again and again in the Quran, and in some places it is a command, as in His saying, Glorious and Exalted is He: And seek forgiveness of Allâh; surely Allâh is Forgiving, Compassionate.

In other places, Allâh praises those who seek His forgiveness, as in the ayah: And those who pray for forgiveness in the early hours of the morning.

Another places, Allâh tells us that He forgives those who ask for His forgiveness, as in the ayah: And whoever does evil, or wrongs his own soul, but afterwards seeks Allâh's forgiveness, will find Allâh is Forgiving, Compassionate.

Seeking forgiveness is frequently associated with repentance, in which case it takes the form of asking for forgiveness with the tongue. Repentance is turning away from wrong actions with both heart and body. Seeking forgiveness is similar to supplication in that Allâh, if He so wishes, responds to it and forgives the person who seeks His forgiveness.

This is especially true if the du 'a came directly from a heart troubled by wrong actions, or if it was made during the times most favorable for His response, such as in the early hours of the morning or immediately following the prayer.

It has been transmitted that Luqman once told his son, "My son, make it a habit for your tongue to utter the words, 'Forgive me, Allâh', for there are certain times during which Allâh will not disappoint a servant who calls on Him."

Al-Hasan said, "Ask for Allâh's forgiveness frequently, in your homes, at your tables, on your roads, in your markets, at your meetings, wherever you are. You never know when you will be granted His forgiveness."

Abu Huraira reported that the Prophet said, "I swear by Allâh that I supplicate for Allâh's forgiveness and turn to Him in repentance more than seventy times a day."

Abu Huraira said, "I heard the Messenger of Allâh say, 'a servant committed a sin and he said, "Allâh, I have committed a sin, so forgive me." Allâh said, "Does My servant know that he has a Lord Who forgives sins and helps him? I forgive My servant." After some time, the man committed another sin so he said, "My Lord, I have committed another sin, so forgive me." His Lord said, "Does My servant know that he has a Lord Who forgives sins and helps him? I forgive My servant." After some time, the man committed yet another sin so he said, "My Lord, I have committed another sin, so forgive me."

His Lord said, "Does My servant know that he has a Lord Who forgives sins and helps him? Servant, do what you like. I have granted you forgiveness.""'

He, Exalted is He, said this three times. This means that the man was granted forgiveness because he continued to seek Allâh's forgiveness each time he committed a sin. It appears that this applied so long as his seeking forgiveness was not accompanied by the intention to repeat the sin again afterwards.

Aisha, may Allâh be pleased with her, said, "It is a fortunate person who (on the Day of judgment) finds in his record many du 'as for forgiveness."

In other words, seeking Allâh's forgiveness is a cure for all wrong actions. Qatada said, "This Quran guides you to the recognition of your illnesses and to their remedies. Your illnesses are your sins and your medicine is seeking Allâh's forgiveness." Ali Ibn Abi Talib, may Allâh be pleased with him, said, "Allâh does not inspire seeking forgiveness in any servant whom He wishes to punish."

"Now await in patience the command of your Lord: for verily you are in Our eyes…"

— Ibn Qayyim al-Jawziyya

Chapter Eight

SUPPLICATION

Allâh, Mighty and Glorious is He, has commanded us to supplicate to Him and has promised to respond to us when we do so. He says:

- Call on Me I will answer you.
- Then He follows this by saying:
- Surely those who are too arrogant to worship Me will enter Hell in humiliation.

Praise be to Allâh, the Most Mighty, Who has boundless generosity and endless mercy. He has made the servant's supplication for the fulfillment of his needs and the accomplishment of his endeavors a rewardable act of worship, which He has asked of him and which He has se- verily reprimanded when he neglects it, by describing him as being arrogant.

Abu Huraira has related that the Prophet said, "Whoever does not supplicate to Allâh invokes His wrath."

He is so right who said: Do not ask the son of Adam to fulfil a need, ask Him whose gates are never concealed. Allâh is wrathful when you do not ask Him, while the son of Adam is angered if you ask him.

Allâh, the Mighty and Glorious, says: Is not He (best) Who answers the one who has been wronged when he calls on Him, and removes the evil?

And also: And when My servants ask you about Me, I am indeed near (to them); I answer the prayer of every supplicant when he calls on Me.

An-Nu'man Ibn Bashir said, "The Messenger of Allâh said, 'Supplication is worship itself.' Then he recited the ayah:

And your Lord has said, 'Call on Me and I will answer you'. Surely those who are too arrogant to worship Me. I will enter Hell in humiliation.

According to the above ayat, any supplication that fulfils the correct requirements will, most surely, be answered by Allâh. This is further confirmed by the following ahadith: "Allâh is the Ever-Living, the Most Generous, and if a man raises his hands in supplication, He will be ashamed to let them be lowered disappointed and empty."

Anas related that the Prophet said, "Do not give up supplicating, for no one who supplicates is ruined."

Abu Sa'id ai-Khudri related that the Prophet said, "No Muslim makes a du'a to Allâh, without being granted one of three things by Allâh: it hastens the fulfilment of what he has asked for; or it is saved up for him until the Day of judgment; or it prevents a similar kind of trouble from happening to him unless it was for something bad, or something that might break family ties."

Omar Ibn ai-Khuttab, may Allâh be pleased with him, said, "I do not have any anxiety about the answer, but I worry about the du'a itself, because anyone who is inspired by Allâh to make du'a 'as immediately invokes His response when he makes the du'a."

Good Observances in Making Supplication

These include choosing the special times for supplicating, such as on the day of Arafat from the days of the year, the month of Ramadan from the months of the year, Friday from among the days of the week, and the early morning hours from the times of the day.

They also include choosing favorable conditions, such as at the time of rain fall, at the time that armies fighting in the way of Allâh march out, and at the time of being in the position of sajdah. Abu Huraira reported that the Prophet said, "A servant is nearest to his Lord when he is in prostration, so increase your supplication when in prostration."

The same applies to the time between the adhan and the iqama. The Messenger of Allâh, may Allâh bless him and grant him peace, said, "Supplication made during the time between the adhan and the iqama is never made in vain."

It is good to be firm when supplicating and confident in Allâh's response. The Prophet said, "None of you should say, 'Allâh, forgive me if You wish' or 'Allâh, have mercy on me if You wish; but he should always be firm in asking Allâh, for nobody can compel Allâh to do something against His will."

It is also good to be in wudu, to be facing towards Makka, and to repeat the du 'a three times.

The supplication should begin with praise of Allâh, by referring to His Names and His Attributes and His blessings, followed by invoking His blessings on the Messenger of Allâh. Then the one who asks should describe his needs and make his requests, and then finally conclude with reciting more prayers on the Prophet. And praise of Allâh, Mighty and Glorious is He.

It is important that his need is pure and that he does not ask for something bad or something that might cause the breaking of family ties.

The one who asks should not insist on the immediate fulfilment of his wishes, nor should he say, "I prayed to Allâh, but He has not responded to my du 'a." Abu Huraira reported that the Prophet said, "The supplication of any one of you will be fulfilled (by Allâh), provided he does not become so impatient as to say, 'I asked, but my request has not been fulfilled.'"

Ibn Battal said, 'What is implied here is that the person despairs and accordingly gives up making du'a altogether in which case it is as if it is he who has condescended to make a du'a, or that he considers his du'a sufficient to war- rant a response, and so he expects an immediate response without any delay from the generous Lord when neither does His responding to du'as diminish His absolute power, nor does His granting His creatures' requests decrease what He has in the least."

This hidith indicates one of the fine courtesies in making du'as, which is that the one who asks should persist and not despair of receiving a positive response to his du'a, for this demonstrates his submission and his absolute reliance on Allâh's assistance.

"If anxiety were to be asked: Who is your father? It would reply: Incapability. On the other hand if competence was asked: Who is your father? It would reply: Steadfastness."

— Ibn Qayyim al-Jawziyya

Chapter Nine

INVOKING BLESSINGS ON THE PROPHET

There is a hadith related by Abu Huraira in which it is reported that the Prophet said, "If anyone invokes blessings on me once, Allâh will grant him ten blessings."

This is because one good deed is recorded as ten good deeds, and invoking blessings on the Prophet is one of the most excellent things a Muslim can do.

Ibn al-Arabi said, "If someone asks about the merit of Allâh's saying Whoever does good shall be given ten times as much. We would say, "It has great merit. The Quran has stated that a good deed is multiplied by ten, and invoking blessings on the Messenger of Allâh is, according to the Quran, a good deed which accordingly gives the one who does it ten grades in the Garden. The Prophet has said that Allâh blesses ten times the one who invokes blessings on him once. Allâh's remembrance of a servant far excels the multiplication of good deeds. This is further supported by the fact that Allâh, Exalted is He, has granted the servant who remembers Him the reward of his being remembered by Him. In the same way, the servant who remembers His Messenger, is rewarded by his being remembered by Him."

Al-Iraqi said, "Allâh's blessing the servant is not his only reward, for, as we are told in the following ahadith, He also records ten good deeds in the servant's record and removes ten wrong actions from it, and raises him up ten levels."

Anas Ibn Malik reported that the Prophet said, "If I am mentioned in anyone's presence then he should invoke blessings on me and if anyone invokes blessings on me once, Allâh will grant him ten blessings." In another version of this hadith the Prophet said, "If anyone invokes blessings on me once, Allâh will grant him ten blessings, wipe out ten of his wrong actions, and raise him up ten levels."

The Prophet's saying, "If I am mentioned in anyone's presence then he should invoke blessings on me", appears to make the invocation of blessings on him obligatory in this situation. There is further proof of this in the hadith, "The miser is the one in whose presence I am mentioned and yet he does not invoke blessings on me."

Ibn Mas'ud reported that the Messenger of Allâh said, "Allâh has roaming angels who come and inform me of the blessings that my Ummah invoke on me.'"

Ibn Mas'ud also reported that the Messenger of Allâh said, "The nearest to me on the Day of Resurrection will be those who invoke blessings on me frequently."

It is best to frequently invoke blessings on the Messenger of Allâh on Fridays. Aws Ibn Aws has related that the Messenger of Allâh said, "Among the most excellent of your days is Friday because on that day Adam was created, and on it he died, and on that day the Trumpet will be sounded, and on it shall come the Hour.

So invoke blessings on me frequently on that day, for your blessings will be brought to me." He was asked, "Messenger of Allâh, how will our blessings be conveyed to you when your body has become part of the decaying earth?" He replied, "Allâh has prohibited the earth from destroying the bodies of the prophets."

As for the form the invocation of blessings on the Prophet should take, Abu Mas'ud Al-Ansari related, "We were sitting in the company of Sa'd Ibn Ubada, when the Messenger of Allâh came to us. Bashir Ibn Sa'd said, 'Messenger of Allâh, Allâh has commanded us to ask blessings on you but how should we invoke blessings on you?' The Messenger of Allâh kept silent. We were much perturbed over his silence and wished that he had not asked him this question. Finally, the Messenger of Allâh said, 'Say, "Allâh, bless Mohamad and the family of Mohamad as You blessed Ibrahim and the family of Ibrahim. Allâh, give baraka to Mohamad and the family of Mohamad as You gave baraka to Ibrahim and the family of Ibrahim. Surely You are worthy of Praise and Glorious," and then give the taslim as you have learnt.'"

"The soul has two forces: the force to proceed and the force to restrain."

— Ibn Qayyim al-Jawziyya

Chapter Ten

TEN PRAYING AT NIGHT

Allâh says: Surely your Lord knows that you stand (in prayer) two thirds of the night, or a half of it, or a third of it.

And also:

And those who spend the night before their Lord, in prostration and standing.

The Prophet: said, "The best prayer, after the obligatory prayers, is the night prayer."

Aisha, may Allâh be pleased with her, said, "Between the 'isha prayer and the fajr prayer, the Prophet, may Allâh bless him and grant him peace, used to pray eleven rak'at. He used to give the taslim after every two rak'at and then pray one witr rak'a."

Ibn Mas'ud related that someone who sleeps throughout the night until dawn (without praying), the Prophet: said, "That is a man in whose ears shaytan urinates."

The Prophet: said, 'When any one of you sleeps, shaytan ties three knots at the back of your head. On each knot he repeats and exhales the following words, 'The night is long, so stay asleep'.

If you wake up and remember Allâh, one knot is undone; and if you do wudu, the second knot is undone; and if you pray, the third knot is undone, and you get up in the morning full of energy and with a clear heart. Otherwise, you get up feeling lazy and with a muddled heart."

Ibn Mas'ud used to get up when other people were asleep, and a continuous humming, like the humming of bees, could be heard coming from him until daybreak.

Al-Hasan was once asked, "How is it that those who stay up at night have the most attractive faces?" He replied, "Because they are on intimate terms with the Merciful, and He robes them in some of His light."

He also said, "A man commits a sin and so (because of it) he is deprived of staying up at night."

A man once said to a righteous man, "I am unable to keep on staying up at night; give me a remedy." The righteous man said, "Do not disobey Him during the day and He will keep you up, between His hands, at night."

It has been transmitted that Suffian ath-Thawri said, "I was once deprived of staying up at night for five months because of a sin that I had committed."

Ibn al-Mubarak said:

When the night is completely dark, it finds them staying up in the night. Fear has chased away their sleep so they stay up, while those who feel secure in this life quietly sleep on.

Ibn Al-Munkadir said, "Only three pleasures remain in this life: staying up at night, meeting one's brothers, and doing the obligatory prayers in jama'a."

"The type medicines that the Prophet SAW and his Companions used to take was nothing like the chemical mixtures that are called Aqrabathayn (pharmacopeia). Rather, the majority of their medicine consisted of only one ingredient. Sometimes, they would take another substance to assist the medicine or make it taste better. This was and still is, the case with most of the medicine used by many cultures such as Arabs, Turks, Indians and nomads."

— Ibn Qayyim al-Jawziyya

Chapter Eleven

DOING WITHOUT THE PLEASURES OF THIS WORLD

Abu'l-Abbas as-Sa'idi said, "A man came to the Prophet: and said, 'Messenger of Allâh! Guide me to such an action that when I do it, Allâh will love me and the people will also love me.' He said, 'be detached from this world and then Allâh will love you, and do not be attached to what people have and then the people will love you.'"

This hadith shows that Allâh loves those who live simply in this life. It has been said that if having love for Allâh is the best state to be in, then living simply is the best condition to be in.

Living simply means that you should restrain your desire for worldly things in the hope of receiving something better instead. In order to achieve this more easily you should first realize that the things which people yearn for in this world are in fact worthless when compared with what we hope for in the next world.

If we know that what Allâh has will remain and that the life to come is better and more lasting, then we realize that the life of this world is really like a piece of ice left out in the sun it soon melts and vanishes. The akhira, however, essentially never vanishes. The desire one has to exchange this life for the one to come is strengthened by the certainty that there is no comparison between this life and the next.

In the Quran we find this world and the next world de- scribed in the following terms: Yes, you prefer the life of this world, but the next world is better and more lasting.

And also: You desire the attractions of this world, but Allâh de- sires the next world for you.

And also: And they are happy with the life of this world, but the life of this world is small comfort compared to the next world.

The ahadith which scorn worldly goods and describe how worthless they are in the sight of Allâh are many: Jabir Ibn Abdullah reported that the Messenger of Allâh: happened to walk through the market place. Some people were gathered on either side of him. There he came across a dead goat with very short ears, of which he took hold, saying, "Who among you would like to have this for a dirham?" They said, "We would not even like to have it for nothing, for it is of no use to us." He said, "Would you like to have it for free?" They said, "By Allâh, not even if it were alive, because its ears are so short; and now it is also dead." Thereupon the Messenger of Allâh: said, "By Allâh, this world is more insignificant in the sight of Allâh than this is in your eyes."

It has been related by Ibn Shaddad al-Fahri that the Prophet: said, "This world, in comparison with the world to come, is the same as if one of you were to put his finger in the ocean. Consider how much you would have when you pulled it out."

It has been related by Ibn Sahl Ibn Sa'ad that the Prophet: said, "Had the world been worth even the wing of a gnat to Allâh, He would not have even given a drink of water from it to a kafir.'"

Living simply means turning away from the things of this world because they are so worthless. You do not bother with them and remain detached from them.

Yunus Ibn Maisarah said, "Being detached from this world does not mean that you should forbid what Allâh has permitted, nor that you should squander money. Rather, it is a state in which you are more certain of what is in the hand of Allâh than you are of what is in your own hands: your state in misfortune is the same as your state at other times; your attitude towards those who quite rightly criticize you and those who quite rightly praise you is the same."

He has explained this in terms of three stages, or stations, all of which are concerned with the heart rather than with physical action. This is why Abu Sulaiman used to say that you should not call anyone a zahid. The first station is that of a servant who is more certain of what is in the hand of Allâh than he is of what is in his own hands. This station arises from a healthy and strong conviction.

Abu-Hazim was asked, "What is your wealth?" He said, "Two kinds of wealth dispel all fear of poverty: trust in Allâh and not being attached to what people have." He was asked, "Don't you fear poverty?" He said, "How can I fear poverty when my Lord owns all that is in the heavens and on the earth and all that is between them and all that is beneath the ground?"

Al-Fudayl said, "The essence of living simply is being content with Allâh, Mighty and Exalted is He." He also said, "The one who is content is the one who lives simply, and it is he who is rich. The one who has attained real faith, who trusts in Allâh in all his affairs, and is content with what He provides for him, and remains unattached to the creation, out of fear and hope and by so doing finds that pursuing worldly gains is not worthwhile has attained the benefits of simplicity. He is the richest of people, even though he may not possess a thing in the word."

As Ammar said, "Death is teacher enough, true faith is wealth enough, and worship is action enough."

Ibn Mas'ud said, "True belief is not trying to please people by doing things which would bring Allâh's displeasure on you; and not envying anyone for what Allâh has given him; and not blaming anyone for what Allâh has not given you. For Allâh's provision is not attracted simply by a man's being careful, nor is it deflected by another man's malice. Allâh, with His justice, Omniscience and Wisdom, has made delight and joy the companions of faith and contentment, and despair and sorrow the companions of dis- trust and dissatisfaction."

The second station is that of a servant who, if he is afflicted by some misfortune like the death of a child, or the loss of wealth or goods desires the reward for his accepting the loss more than his recovering what has been lost. This is also a consequence of having complete trust. Ali, may Allâh be pleased with him, said, "Whoever lives simply in this world finds misfortunes easy to endure."

Some of our predecessors used to say, "If it were not for the misfortunes of this world, we would arrive in the next world completely destitute."

The third station is that of a servant who regards praise and criticism equally. If the world occupies a place of importance in his heart, then he would prefer praise to blame, which in turn might make him abandon much good for fear of being censured, and do many bad things in his quest for praise. This means that in his heart other people's opinions about him are of no importance to him indeed what is important to him is his love of the Truth and his earning Allâh's good pleasure.

Ibn Mas'ud said, "True faith is not trying to please other people by doing things which are displeasing to Allâh." Allâh has praised those who fight in His way, without worrying about the opinions of others.

Al-Hasan said, "The person who lives simply is the one who finds it in his heart to say that someone else has surpassed him in it." Imam Ahmad, I believe, was once asked whether a wealthy man could live simply. He said, "Yes, if he is not pleased when his wealth increases, nor sad when it decreases, then he can."

Ibrahim Ibn Adham said, "There are three types of zhud, or doing without: the first is as a result of having to do so, the second of praiseworthy action, and the third of being careful. Avoiding haram things is obligatory, avoiding things which are halal may be praiseworthy, and avoiding things which are doubtful is prudent."

Any person who exchanges the things of this world for the next world is doing without something in this life and so we can call him a zahid, but doing without can also involve enjoying something m this world at the expense of the next world; in this case it is something in the akhira with which one is doing without.

A righteous man was once told, "You do without much more than I do." The man replied, "It is you who are more extreme in this, for I deny myself things in a life which will not last and whose rewards are uncertain, while you have denied yourself the akhira. No one could be more extreme in their doing without than this."

Normally, however, when we speak of zuhud we mean that we deny ourselves some of the pleasures of this world rather than those of the next world. However it is only possible to abstain from things to which you have access. This is why Ibn al-Mubarak said, when someone said to him, "Zahid!", "The real zahid is Omar Ibn Abdai-Aziz, for he rejected the tremendous pleasures and riches of this world that were placed at his feet, whereas I have very little to give up."

Al-Hasan al-Basri said, "I have known people and kept company with groups who neither rejoiced when the things of this world came to them, nor grieved when they lost anything in this world. The life of this world was more insignificant to them than dust. One of them might live for a year or for sixty years without ever having a garment that would entirely cover him, and without ever having anything that would come between him and the ground, and without ever having any food that he could ask to be prepared for him in his own home.

"When night came, they would be on their feet, with their foreheads flat against the earth, tears rolling down their cheeks, secretly calling on Allâh to save them on the Day of Judgment. If they did something good, they never stopped being grateful for it, and were always asking Allâh to accept it. If they did something bad, they would be saddened by it, and would keep on asking Allâh to forgive them for it. By Allâh, they were not safe from wrong actions, and were saved only by their constant turning in repentance. May Allâh be pleased with them and grant them His mercy."

There are three stages of zuhud: The first stage is to withdraw from the life of this world, even though you may still have a great desire for it and your heart is still drawn towards it. The self is still pre-occupied with the world, even though you struggle with it and restrain it.

The second stage is to acquire detachment from this world and to do without in it, in order to obtain your re- ward for avoiding it. Here, it is your doing without which preoccupies you. This is the state of the person who gives away a dirham in order to obtain two.

The third stage is that of the one who willingly puts the world to one side without even a thought for what he has abandoned. This is the one who has exchanged a fragment of broken pottery for a jewel. Or it is like someone who, seeking to gain entrance to see the King, may be prevented by a dog at the gate. By throwing the dog a scrap it is distracted, and this makes it possible for him to gain entrance to the King's audience chamber. Shaytan is like that dog, standing at the gates of Allâh. He tries to prevent people from entering them, even though the gates are wide open and the world is just a scrap which you can toss aside without a second thought.

"Crying out and complaining to Allâh does not mean that a person has no patience.

In the Qur'ân, we find Ya'qûb, peace be upon him, saying: "My course is comely patience (sabrun jamîl)" (Yûsuf 12:83), but his love and longing for his lost son Yûsuf made him say: "How great is my grief for Yûsuf" (Yûsuf 12:83).

Sabrun jamîl refers to patience with no complaint to other people. Complaining to Allâh does not cancel out patience, as Ya'qûb said: "I only complain of my distraction and anguish to Allâh" (Yûsuf 12:86)."

— Ibn Qayyim al-Jawziyya

Chapter Twelve

THE STATES OF THE SELF

There is agreement amongst those who seek Allâh, despite their different schools and practices that the self stands between the heart and reaching Him. Only the silencing of the self by turning away from it and ignoring its whims and overcoming it can lead you into the domain of Allâh and make it possible to reach Him.

There are two kinds of people: one kind are those whose nafs have overcome them and led them to ruin because they yielded to them and obeyed their impulses. The other kind are those who have overcome their nafs and made them obey their commands.

Some of those who know have said, "The journey of those who seek Allâh ends with them overcoming their selves, because whoever triumphs over his self succeeds and wins, and whoever has his self-triumph over him loses."

Allâh, the Exalted, says: Then as for whoever exceeded the limits and preferred the life of this world, surely his abode will be the Fire; and as for whoever feared to stand before his Lord and restrained the desires of his self, surely his abode will be the Garden.

The self urges you to wrong actions, and to preferring this life to the next life; while Allâh tells his servants to fear Him, and to restrain the self from following its impulses. The heart is torn between these two. It listens to one caller one moment and to the other caller the next. Here lies the source of affliction, and a challenge.

In the Quran, Allâh has described three states of the self: the self at peace, the reproachful self, and the self that urges evil. Accordingly, people have varied in their views as to whether a servant has one self, of which these three states are attributes, or three selves.

The first view is that of the people of knowledge and explanation, while the second has been attributed to the Sufis. The truth of the matter is that there is no contradiction between the two. The self is a single entity as far as its essence is concerned, and is one of three main types, depending on what attributes it has.

The Self at Peace

When the self can rest at peace in the Presence of Allâh, and is made tranquil when His Name is invoked, and always relates all matters to Him, and often turns to Him, and is impatient to meet Him, and experiences the intimacy of His nearness, then this is a soul at peace.

It is the soul to whom it is said at the time of death: O soul at peace, return to your Lord, well pleased and well-pleasing. Enter with My servants, enter into My Garden.

Ibn al-Abbas, may Allâh be pleased with him, said, "It is the tranquil and believing soul."

Qatada said, "It is the soul of the believer, made calm by what Allâh has promised. Its owner is at complete rest and content with his knowledge of Allâh's Names and At- tributes, and with what He has said about Himself and His Messenger, may Allâh bless him and grant him peace, and with what He has said about what awaits the soul after death about the departure of the soul, the life in the bar- zakh, and the events of the Day of Resurrection which will follow so much so that a believer such as this can almost see them with his own eyes. So he submits to the will of Allâh and surrenders to Him contentedly, never dissatisfied or complaining, and with his faith never wavering. He does not rejoice at his gains, nor do his afflictions make him despair, for he knows that they were decreed long be- fore they happened to him, even before he was created, for Allâh says: No calamity occurs without the permission of Allâh; and whoever trusts in Allâh, He guides his heart; and Allâh knows all things."

Many of our predecessors have said that such a soul be- longs to the servant who, when afflicted by misfortune, knows that it is from Allâh and accepts it and submits to His will. The peace that comes with ihsan springs from a reassuring familiarity with the decree of Allâh, which is reflected in submission, sincerity and worship.

No desire, or will, or force of habit, can be given precedence over His will and command; there can be no attraction to anything that contradicts any of His Attributes; and there can be no desire that opposes His decree and if ever such a thing does happen to such a person, then he simply dismisses it as the whispering of shaytan. Indeed he would rather fall from the sky than give reality to such a thing within himself.

This, as the Prophet said, is dear and true faith.' By it he is saved from the worry that accompanies wrong actions and from any anxiety about them, thanks to the peace and sweetness that come with turning to Him.

If he comes to rest in firm belief after having doubted, or in knowledge after ignorance, or in remembrance after being forgetful, or in repentance after rebellion, or in sincerity after showing off, or in truthfulness after deceit, or in clarity after confusion, or in the humility of intimacy after the impetuousness of desire, or in modesty after boastfulness, then his soul is at peace.

All this is due to the awareness that frees the heart from idle sleep and lights up the palaces of the Garden ahead of him as when a man cried out: O soul, watch out' Help me with your striving in the darkness of the nights, so that on the Day of Resurrection you will win a good life on those heights!

He recognized, by the light of this awakening, what he had been created for, and what he would encounter, from the moment he died to the moment he entered the abode that lasts forever (i.e. the Garden or the Fire). He realized how swiftly this world passes, and how unreliable it is for its children, and how it destroys whoever loves it. So he arose in this light, full of determination and said:

Ah, woe is me, that I was forgetful of Allâh!

So he sets out on a fresh start in his life, making up for what he has missed and bringing back to life what had died. Now he faces the pitfalls that he encountered before head-on, and seizes the moment with his newly discovered capacity, which, when it passed him by before, caused him to miss all good.

Then he realizes, in the light of this awakening and in the light of Allâh's gifts to him, that he is incapable of measuring and counting Allâh's blessings, or of repaying his debt. With this realization, he recognizes his shortcomings and faults, his wrong actions and all the bad things he has done, all of his disobedience and the neglect of so many rights and duties. His self is broken and his body is humbled and he approaches Allâh with his head down. He recognizes Allâh's generosity and sees his own misdeeds and faults both at the same time.

He also sees, in the light of this awakening, how precious his time is, and how important it is. He realizes that it is the capital of his future well-being which must not be wasted, and he becomes so thrifty with it that he only spends it in actions and deeds which will bring him nearer to Allâh •for wasting time is the seed of failure and regret, and being careful with it is the root of success and joy.

These then, are the consequences of being aware and what increase it. These are the first steps of the soul at peace on its journey to Allâh and the akhira.

The Reproachful Self

It has been said that this kind of self is the one which cannot rest in any one state. It often changes and alters, re- members and forgets, submits and evades, loves and hates, rejoices and becomes sad, accepts and rejects, obeys and rebels.

It has also been said that it is the self of the believer. Al-Hasan al-Basri said, "You always see the believer reproaching himself and saying things like: 'Did I want this? Why did I do that? Was this better than that?'"

It has also been said that the self blames itself on the Day of Resurrection: every one blames himself for his actions, either for his bad deeds, if he was one who had many wrong actions, or for his short comings, if he was one who did good deeds.

Imam Ibn al-Qayyim says that all of this is accurate. There are two types of reproachful self: one that is blameworthy and one that is not blameworthy. The blame worthy self is the ignorant, disobedient self that Allâh and His angels blame. The self that is not blameworthy is the self that blames its owner for his own shortcomings in obeying Allâh, in spite of all his efforts in that direction. This self is not really blameworthy.

The most praiseworthy selves are the ones that blame themselves because of their shortcomings in obeying Allâh. This is the self that endures criticism from others in its quest to please Him, so that no one can find fault with it as regards his worship of Him. This one has escaped being blamed by Allâh.

As for the self which accepts its actions as they are, without self-criticism, and which does not have to endure the criticisms of others which means that it cannot be being sincerely obedient to Allâh this is the self that Allâh blames.

The Self that Urges Evil

This is the self that brings punishment on itself. By its very nature it directs its owner towards every wrong action. No one can be rid of its evil without help from Allâh.

As Allâh says of the wife of al-Aziz, in the story of Yusuf: And I do not say that my self is free from blame: surely the self urges evil, unless my Lord is Merciful; surely my Lord is Forgiving, Compassionate.

Allâh also says: And had it not been for the grace of Allâh and His Mercy on you, not one of you would ever have been pure; but Allâh purifies whomever He wishes, and Allâh is Hearing, Knowing.

We have been taught the du 'a, "All praise is for Allâh, we praise Him and seek His help and His pardon. We seek refuge in Him from the evil in ourselves and from the evil of our deeds."

Evil lies hiding in the self, and it is this that leads it on to do wrong. If Allâh were to leave the servant alone with his self, the servant would be destroyed between its evil and the evil that it craves; but if Allâh grants him success and help, then he will survive. We seek refuge in Allâh the Almighty, both from the evil of ourselves and from the evil of our deeds.

So the self is a single entity, although its state may change: from the self that urges evil, an-nafs al-ammara, to the reproachful self, an-nafs al-lawwama, to the self at peace, an-nafs al-mutim'inna, which is the final aim of perfection. The self at peace has an angel to help it, who assists and guides it. The angel casts good into the self, so that it desires what is good and is aware of the excellence of good actions. The angel also keeps the self away from wrong action and shows it the ugliness of bad deeds.

All in all, whatever is for Allâh and by Him, always comes from the soul which is at peace. The self which urges evil has shaytan as its ally. He promises it great rewards and gains, but casts falsehood into it. He invites it and entices it to do evil. He leads it on with hope after hope and presents falsehood to it in a form that it will accept and admire.

The nafs al-mutma'inna, the self at peace, and its angel require the following: unwavering belief in Allâh, the One, without any partner; moral excellence; good behavior towards Allâh, and parents, and companions, and so on; fear of Allâh; total reliance on Allâh; turning in repentance to Allâh; relating all things to Allâh; drawing near to Allâh; curbing expectations; and being prepared for death and what follows it.

Shaytan and his helpers, on the other hand, require the nafs al-ammara, the self that urges evil the opposite of all this. The most difficult challenge to the self at peace is to free itself from the influence of shaytan and the nafs al-ammara. If it undertakes this struggle, then it becomes nafs al-lawwama, the reproachful self; and if the struggle is won, then it be- comes nafs al-mutma 'inna. If even one good action were to be accepted by Allâh, one would have success by virtue of it, but shaytan and the nafs al-ammara refuse to urge the self to do even one such deed.

Some of those who were given knowledge of Allâh and of their own selves have said, "If I could know for certain that even one of my actions had been accepted by Allâh, then I would be happier at the arrival of death than the much travelled wayfarer is at the sight of his family."

Abdullah Ibn Omar said, "If I could know for certain that Allâh had accepted even one of my prostrations, there would be no long lost friend dearer to me than death itself."

The nafs al-ammara urges evil and openly opposes the nafs al-mutma'inna. Whenever the latter presents a good deed, the former presents an evil deed in return. The nafs al-ammara tells the nafs al-mutma'inna that jihad is nothing more than suicide, a widowed wife, orphaned children, and wasted wealth. It tries to convince the nafs al-mutma'inna that zakat and sadaqa are nothing less than an unnecessary expense and a burden, a hole in your pocket, which will lead you to depend on others, so that you too will then be like the poor.

Bringing the Self to Account

When the self that urges evil overwhelms the heart of a believer, the only remedy is to bring it to account and then to disregard it. Imam Ahmad has related on the authority of Omar Ibn ai-Khuttab, may Allâh be pleased with him, that the Prophet, may Allâh bless him and grant him peace, said, "The intelligent person is the one who brings his self to account and acts in preparation for what lies beyond his death; and the foolish person is the one who abandons himself to his desires and cravings and expects Allâh to fulfil his futile wishes."

Imam Ahmad also related that Omar Ibn ai-Khuttab, may Allâh be pleased with him, said, "Judge your selves before you yourselves are judged; and weigh your selves in the balance before you yourselves are weighed in the balance. When you are brought to account tomorrow, it will be much easier for you if you have already brought your selves to account today so do so, before you come to the Final Gathering for:

• On that Day you will be exposed whatever you have hidden will no longer be hidden."

Al-Hasan said, "A believer is responsible for his self, and he brings it to account in order to please Allâh. Judgment will be lighter on the Day of Judgment for the people who have brought their selves to account in this life, but it will be severe for the people who did not prepare for it by bringing their selves to account beforehand."

A believer is distracted by something that he likes, so he says to it: "By Allâh, I like you and I need you, but there is no means by which I can have you, so you have been kept from me." When whatever it is, is out of his sight and beyond his reach, then he returns to his senses and says, "I did not really want this! What made me preoccupied with it? By Allâh, I shall never concern myself with it again!"

The believers are a people who have been prevented through the Quran from indulging in the pleasures of this world; it comes between them and what might destroy them.

The believer is like a prisoner in this world, who tries to free himself from its shackles and fetters, placing his trust in nothing in it, until the day he meets his Creator. He knows full well that he is accountable for every- thing that he hears, sees and says, and for everything that he does with his body.

Malik Ibn Dinar said, "May Allâh grant mercy to a servant who says to his self, 'Aren't you such and such? Didn't you do such and such?' Then he rebukes it and puts it in its place, and disciplines it and restrains it in accordance with the Book of Allâh, Mighty and Glorious is He, and becomes its guide and master."

It is undoubtedly the responsibility of anyone who believes in Allâh and the Day of Judgment, and who wishes to keep his affairs in order, to make sure that he brings his self to account. He must control what it does and what it does not do, even its most insignificant activities, for each and every breath you take during your life-time is precious. It can be used to acquire one of the treasures which ensure a state of bliss that is everlasting. Whoever wastes it, or uses it to acquire things which may cause his destruction, will suffer great losses, which are only allowed to happen by the most ignorant, foolish and reckless of people. The true extent of such losses will only become apparent on the Day of Judgment. Allâh, Exalted is He, says:

• On the Day when every soul will be confronted with all the good that it has done and all the evil that it has done, it will wish that there were a great distance be- tween it and its evil.

There are two ways of bringing the self to account: one precedes action, the other follows it. The first way is the decision that is made when a believer hesitates before acting. This is the moment of evaluation before intention is formed. He does not proceed until he is sure that it is good and sound. If it is not, then he abandons it. Al-Hasan, may Allâh be pleased with him, said, "May Allâh grant mercy to a servant who hesitates at the point of evaluation, and then if he sees that the action is for Allâh, he carries on with it, but if he sees that it for some- thing other than Allâh, then he holds back from completing it."

This has been explained as meaning that when the self-first feels like doing something or other, and the servant begins by considering its worth, he first stops and thinks to himself, "Can I do this?" If the answer is no, he will not undertake the action. If it is yes, he will again stop and ask himself, "Is it better for me to do it than not to do it?" If the answer is no, he will abandon it and not attempt to do it, but if the answer is yes, he will then pause for a third time and ask himself, "Is this action motivated by the desire to seek Allâh's pleasure and reward, or is It in order to ac- quire power, admiration, and money?"

If it is the latter that has prompted the idea of the action, then he will not undertake it, even if it would result in his acquiring those worldly gains which prompted the idea of the action in the first place for otherwise this would result in his self-becoming accustomed to associating others with Allâh, and it would make acting for the sake of something or someone other than Allâh easier for it, and the easier it is to do things for other than Him, the harder it becomes to do things that are intended for His pleasure.

If it is the former that has prompted the idea of the action, he stops yet again and asks himself, "Will I receive help in doing this? Do I have any companions who will help me and come to my assistance if I need their help in undertaking this action?" If he finds that he has no allies to help him, he will hold back from going through with this action, just as the Prophet held back from waging the jihad against the Makkans until he had enough allies and sufficient forces to ensure success.

If he finds that there is assistance on which he can rely in undertaking the proposed action, then at last he should start doing it, and he will succeed, by the will of Allâh. Failure can only occur if one of these safeguards is lacking, for when they are all combined together they guarantee success. These are the four steps that a servant needs to take in bringing his self to account before he does anything.

The second way is that of bringing the self to account after an action. There are three categories of this: First, bringing the self to account for an act of obedience in which what is due to Allâh has not been completely fulfilled or done in the best possible way. There are six things that are due to Allâh in acts of obedience: Sincerity in doing it, devoting it to Allâh only, following the example of the Prophet, paying attention to doing it well, recognizing Allâh's blessings in it, and, after all this, being aware of your own shortcomings in how you do it. A person brings his self to account, but has he given ell these prerequisites their due attention and effort? Did he fulfill them in his act of obedience?

Second, bringing the self to account for any action which would have been better left undone than done.

Third, bringing the self to account as to whether or not the intention in undertaking a permitted action was to seek the pleasure of Allâh, Exalted is He, and success in the akhira, thereby guaranteeing successor was it in fact to seek the fleeting gains of this life, thereby losing what could have otherwise been gained.

The last thing a person should do is to be inattentive and neglectful in bringing his self to account, by starting out without any preparation, and by treating matters lightly and just muddling along. This will only bring about his ruin. This is the destiny of the people who are arrogant.

Such a one turns a blind eye to the consequences of acting like this and relies on Allâh's forgiveness. He neglects bringing his self to account and does not contemplate the outcome of his behavior. If he does not do this, then he easily falls into wrong actions, until he becomes accustomed to them, and then finds it difficult to pull himself away from them.

All in all, the believer should first bring his self to ac- count as regards his obligatory acts of worship. If he finds himself lacking in these, then he should hasten to rectify his situation, either by catching up with the worship he has neglected, or by correcting whatever he may have been doing wrong in his worship.

Next, he should bring his self to account as regards acts which are forbidden. If he finds that he has done any of them, he must quickly turn in repentance, seek Allâh's forgiveness, and do good deeds in order to eradicate the bad deeds which have been recorded in his record.

Next, he should bring his self to account as regards those matters in which he has been negligent. If he finds that he has been negligent in doing what he was created for, he should hasten to the remembrance of Allâh and drawing near to Him with an open heart.

Next, he should bring his self to account for the words he has spoken, for the steps his feet have taken, for the things his hands have grasped, and for what his ears have listened to. He should ask himself, "What did I want this for? What did I do that for? Whom did I do this for? Why did I do it like that?"

He should know that every action and every word are accounted for in two books; one is entitled, "For whom did I do it?", and the other, "How well did I do it?" The first question is concerned with sincerity, and the second is concerned with the action itself. Allâh, the Exalted, says:

• That He may question the truthful about their truthfulness.

If the truthful ones are going to be asked about their truthfulness, and will be judged in accordance with how truthful they were, what do you imagine will be the case with the people of falsehood?

The Merits of Bringing the Soul to Account

This involves:

First, identifying the faults of the self. Whoever does not recognize his faults cannot possibly get rid of them. Yunus Ibn Ubaid said, "I know about a hundred of the attributes of goodness and yet I cannot find even one of them in myself."

Muhammed Ibn Wasi said, "If wrong actions produced flatulence, no one would have been able to sit in my company."

Imam Ahmad wrote that Abu'd-Darda' said, "No man gains full understanding and knowledge unless he detests all the people who are not close to Allâh, and then turns his attention to his own self and detests it even more."

Second, knowing what rights are due to Allâh. This is important because it makes the servant detest his self and frees him from arrogance and being self-satisfied with his actions. This opens the doors of submission and humility for him, and results in the purification of his soul at the hands of his Lord. He despairs for his self and believes firmly that his survival will not be achieved without the forgiveness, generosity and mercy of Allâh. It is His right to be constantly obeyed, remembered and thanked.

"Whosoever wishes that his vision be truthful must seek to attain truthfulness, consume nothing but what is lawful, hold fast to the commandments and prohibitions. Furthermore, he should sleep in the state of ritual purity, face the Qibla and mention God until overtaken by sleep. The vision of such a one is seldom false. In addition, the most truthful of visions are those seen in the early morning [before dawn], as that is the time of divine descent, and proximity of mercy and forgiveness, respite from the devils. Its opposite is the vision seen in the early part of the night when the devils and devilish souls are spread about."

— Ibn Qayyim al-Jawziyya

Chapter Thirteen
PERSEVERANCE

Allâh has made perseverance a tireless horse, a relentless cutting sword, an invincible, victorious army, an indestructible, formidable fortress. It and victory are inseparable companions.

Allâh, Mighty and Glorious is He, has praised those who persevere in His Book, and says that He gives them endless rewards and supports them with His guidance, might and a clear victory. He says:

• And be patient surely Allâh is with those who are patient.

By virtue of this companionship, those who persevere gain both in this life and in the next life as they deserve; they win both His evident and hidden blessings.

Allâh has made leadership in the deen dependent on perseverance and certainty. He says:

• And We appointed leaders from among them who guided by Our command, so long as they persevered and firmly believed in Our Signs.

And He says that the perseverance of those who persevere is good for them, and He has affirmed this with an oath:

- And if you persevere, that is indeed better for those who persevere.

And He says that through perseverance and fear of Allâh, the schemes of the enemy will not cause His faithful servants any harm, even if they are of the worst kind:

- And if you persevere and have taqwa, their cunning will not harm you at all surely Allâh surrounds what- ever they do.

Allâh has made success conditional on perseverance and righteousness:

- You who believe, persevere, and be patient, and hold together firmly, and fear Allâh, so that you may be successful.

He also speaks of His love for those who persevere, which is the greatest incentive possible for anyone who seeks His love:

- And Allâh loves those who persevere.

Allâh gives good news to those who persevere and promises them three things, each of which is far better than anything the people of this world envy one another for:

• And give good news to those who persevere, those who say, when a misfortune strikes them, "Surely we come from Allâh, and surely to Him we return"; these are the ones on whom blessings from their Lord descend, and mercy, and these are the ones who are rightly guided.

Allâh has made the attainment of a place in the Garden and the avoidance of a place in the Fire the exclusive re- ward of those who patiently persevere:

• Surely I have rewarded them this Day for their patience and surely they are the ones who are successful.

By making them the particular beneficiaries of His ayat, Allâh has distinguished those who endure and persevere and are grateful for such great good fortune. He says, in four different places in the Quran:

Surely in this there are signs for everyone who perseveres and gives thanks.

Perseverance is a true attribute of the believer. He or- des round it and then returns to it. It is the pillar that sup- ports his faith, without which he could not remain upright. Whoever has no perseverance can have no faith, or if he does have some faith, then it is scant and weak. Such a person worships Allâh half-heartedly: if he encounters good in this life, he is reassured in his belief, but if he is afflicted by misfortune, then he turns away from Allâh and loses everything both in this life and in the next life, settling for a losing deal.

The good news proclaimed by the Prophet Jesus, peace be on him, was only appreciated by the fortunate ones be- cause of their perseverance, and they ascended to the highest ranks because of their gratitude. They flew with the wings of perseverance and gratitude to the Gardens of Bliss:

Race with each other towards forgiveness from your Lord and a Garden whose extent is like the extent of the heavens and the earth which is in store for those who believe in Allâh and His messengers. That is Allâh's grace which He grants to whomever He wishes and Allâh's grace is vast.

Since perseverance and gratitude are two elements of faith, whoever is concerned about the well-being of his soul desiring its salvation and hoping for its good fortune must not neglect these two essentials.

He must approach Allâh with them, so that He may put him among those who are successful on the Day that he meets Him.

The Meaning and Essence of Perseverance

The word sabr in Arabic, meaning 'perseverance' or 'patience', indicates holding back and self-restraint. In the context of the shari'ah, it means keeping the self from being agitated, the tongue from complaining, and the hands from beating cheeks and tearing clothes (as an expression of grief).

It has been said that it is one of the excellent possessions of the self, without which it is not possible to do any-thing well. It is a strength of the self that makes it possible to put it right and benefit it.

When Imam Junaid was asked what it is, he said, "Swallowing something bitter without displaying any dis-taste on your face."

Dhu'n-Nun al-Misri said of it, "Perseverance is distancing yourself from all wrongs and transgressions, and remaining calm when you are engulfed by impossible afflictions, and appearing to have enough when poverty is in permanent residence in your home."

It has also been said that perseverance is, "Standing firm and remaining courteous when affliction strikes, and remaining content when afflicted with misfortune, without showing any signs of complaint."

One day, a righteous man saw someone complaining to his brother, so he said to him, "By Allâh what you are really doing is complaining about the One Who is merciful to you, as you complain to one who has no mercy of his own to give to you."

It has also been said: When you complain to the son of Adam, you are in fact complaining about the Merciful to one who has no mercy of his own.

There are two types of complaint:

The first type of complaint is a complaining to Allâh, Mighty and Glorious is He, which is not inconsistent with perseverance, as in the saying of the Prophet Ya'qub, peace be on him, when he said:

"I only reveal my distress and sorrow to Allâh."

And also: "So patience is beautiful."

The Prophet: said, "Allâh! I complain to You about the weakness of my strength and the lack of my ability."

The second type of complaint is a complaining about affliction, by objecting to its nature and character. This kind is incompatible with perseverance and it contradicts it and cancels it out.

The arena of power is more significant for the servant than the arena of perseverance; as the Prophet: said to Allâh, "If You are not angry with me, I will not be concerned, but Your Might is more significant for me."

This does not contradict his: saying, "No one has been given a better or greater gift than perseverance."

This applies to someone who has been afflicted by a misfortune. The arena of perseverance in his case is the greatest one, but, before affliction strikes, the arena of strength and health is more significant.

The self is the riding beast that carries the servant either to the Garden or to the Fire. Perseverance is to the self what the reins and blinkers are to the riding beast if it had neither, it would wander off in all directions.

Al-Hajjaj once said, "Keep your selves in check, for they can get up to all sorts of mischief. May Allâh grant mercy to whom-ever puts reins and blinkers on his self, directing it with the blinkers towards obedience to Allâh, and steering it away from disobedience with the reins. Patiently avoiding what Allâh has forbidden is easier than enduring the punishment that He inflicts."

There are two types of impetus that drive the self: one is the active impulse of courage, and the other is the inhibiting force of restraint.

The true essence of perseverance is to chanel the first type of energy towards what is beneficial, and to use the second type of energy to avoid doing what is harmful.

There are people who persevere in doing the night prayer regularly and in enduring the burden of fasting, and yet they do not have the power to refrain from a forbidden glance. There are others who can do this, and yet they do not have the energy to persevere in enjoining good and forbidding evil, or in fighting a jihad.

It has been said, "Endurance, patience, and perseverance are what constitute the bravery of the self." Similar to this saying is the proverb, "Courage is being able to persevere for a while."

Enduring patiently is the opposite of being agitated. As Allâh, Mighty and Glorious is He, says of the people of the Fire and what they say:

Whether we rage, or patiently endure, is the same for us (now) for us there is no way of escape.

Types of Courage and Being a Good Servant

There are three kinds of courage or perseverance, depending on the intention behind it: perseverance in completing acts of worship and being obedient; perseverance in refraining from forbidden actions and being disobedient; and perseverance in the face of destiny so that the servant does not become angry in times of adversity.

It has been said about these different types, "A servant must have a command to obey, prohibitions to avoid, and adversity to endure."

There is another way of categorizing endurance and perseverance, namely, perseverance where there is a choice and perseverance where there is no choice. The former is better and has greater significance than the latter, for perseverance where there is no choice is the kind which is common to all people; it is exercised by all those who do not display perseverance by choice.

For this reason the perseverance of the Prophet Yusuf, peace be on him, in refusing the advances of the wife of Al-Aziz is more significant than his enduring what his brothers inflicted on him when they threw him in the well.

Man can never do without perseverance. He fluctuates between a command that he must obey and fulfil, prohibitions he must avoid and do without, destiny which must run its course, and blessings for which he must thank the Provider. As the human situation never changes, man ha' to persevere until the day he dies.

Everything that the servant meets in this life is one of two kinds: one kind matches his desires and accords with his wishes, while the other does not. He needs to have patience for both kinds, but the first kind such as having health, wealth and power requires more patience from him in several respects:

First, he should not place his confidence in them; nor should he be arrogant and bad mannered because of them; nor should they be the cause of his being ungrateful; nor should he celebrate with them in ways of which Allâh does not approve.

Second, he should not become preoccupied with acquiring them.

Third, he must persevere in fulfilling what is due to Allâh in them. Fourth, he must persist in his efforts not to expend them in making haram profits.

It has been said, "Both the mumin and the kafir are able to persevere in times of hardship, but only the truly faithful are capable of persevering in times of ease."

Abdur-Rahman Ibn Awf said, "We were afflicted with hardship, and we persevered and •endured, but when we enjoyed times of ease, we were unable to persevere." That is why Allâh warns His servants against becoming engrossed or preoccupied with money, spouses and children. He says, Mighty and Exalted is He: you who believe, do not let your wealth or your children distract you from the remembrance of Allâh.

The other kind, which does not accord with his desires and wishes, is either related to matters where the servant has a choice such as acts of obedience or disobedience or with matters in which the servant has no choice such as afflictions. Perhaps he has a choice in the very beginning, but not in ending them once they are under way.

Thus of this second kind there are three categories: First, there are matters in which the servant has a choice, which include all the actions involving either obedience or disobedience.

In the case of actions involving obedience, the servant needs to persevere in doing them because the self, by its very nature, dislikes much of what is involved in worship and service. In doing the prayer, for example, the self is lazy and prefers taking it easy, especially if it is accompanied by a hardened heart that has been overwhelmed by wrong action, and is inclined to follow its own desires and mix with people who neglect Allâh's commands. In paying zakat, perseverance and endurance are needed because of the mean and miserly characteristics of the self.

In doing the hajj and fighting jihad, perseverance is required, because of both of the above mentioned characteristics combined: laziness and meanness.

A servant needs to persevere in three circumstances: First, before fulfilling an act of obedience, by paying attention to his sincerity in doing this act of obedience. Second, during the act of obedience, by persisting in completing it without any omissions and without being negligent, in accordance with his sincere intentions, and without allowing the physical performance of the action to distract his heart from being at rest in full submission be- fore Allâh, the Exalted.

Third, after completing the act of obedience by patiently avoiding anything that might wipe out its reward. This kind of patience means that he must not be pleased with his having been obedient and boast about it, bringing it out from the realm of the veiled secret in to that of public scrutiny.

The act of the servant is a secret between himself and Allâh, the Exalted, and it is recorded as such in the realm of secrets. If he talks about it, it is removed from there to the reality' of public knowledge. So he must not think that there is no more need for perseverance once the physical action has been completed.

In the case of acts of disobedience, the matter is clear and simple. The greatest help for the servant in patiently avoiding such acts is to give up his bad habits and to avoid contact with those who encourage such habits through companionship and conversation.

Second, there are matters in which the servant has no choice, and which he has no means of avoiding, such as misfortunes, which either are not of man's own making like death and illness or are caused by man like physical violence and verbal abuse.

In relation to the First kind of misfortune, there are four known stations: the station of inability to cope, which include being agitated and complaining; the station of patient endurance and perseverance; the station of acceptance and contentment; and the station of gratitude, in which the misfortune is viewed as a blessing and so the one who is afflicted is thankful to the One Who Afflicts him for it.

In relation to the second kind of misfortune, which is caused by man. There are these four stations, plus four more: the station of forgiveness; the station of clarity of the heart regarding any wish to satisfy any desire for revenge; the station of being in a position to do so; and the station of treating the wrongdoer with kindness.

Third, there are matters which are brought about by the servant's own choice, but once they have happened and taken hold of his situation, he is left with no choice in being able to change them or to free himself from their effects on him.

Merits of Courage and Perseverance

Umm Salama, may Allâh be pleased with her, reported that she heard the Messenger of Allâh: say, "There is no Muslim who, when afflicted with a misfortune, says as Allâh has ordered him to say, Surely to Allâh we belong, and surely to Him we are returning, Allâh, reward me in my misfortune and give me better than it afterwards', except that Allâh grants him better than it."

She continued, "When Abu Salama died, I said, 'which one of the Muslims is better than Abu Salama, whose family was the first to follow the Messenger of Allâh: in making hijra?' Then I said what Allâh has ordered us to say, and He gave me marriage to His Messenger.'"

Abu Huraira has related that the Messenger of Allâh: said, "The Mighty and Glorious says, 'I have nothing but the Garden as a reward for My faithful servant who, when I take back one of the most excellent people of this world through death), remains patient and hopes for Allâh's reward.'"

In the two books of as-Sahih, it is reported that Aisha, may Allâh be pleased with her, related that the Messenger of Allâh: said, "Any believer who is afflicted by a misfortune, even if it is as little as the prick of a thorn, will have it removed from his record of wrong actions, in return for it."

Abu Huraira reported that the Prophet: said, "The believer continues to be afflicted with hardships in his or her body, wealth and children, until he or she meets Allâh completely free of all wrong actions." Khabbab Ibn Ai-Arath reported, "We complained to the Messenger of Allâh: about our situation while he was lying in the shade of the Ka'aba, with his head resting on his cloak. We said, 'Will you ask Allâh to help us? Will you invoke Allâh for us?'

"He said, 'Among those who were before you, a believer used to be seized and placed in a pit dug especially for him; then a saw would be brought and put on his head which would then be cut into two halves, after his flesh had been sliced with iron combs and torn from his bones and yet all that did not make him abandon his deen. By Allâh! this deen will be completed, and a rider will be able to travel from San'a to Hadramout, fearing nobody except Allâh and the wolf lest it should trouble his sheep but you are impatient!'" '

Some of our predecessors used to say, "Had it not been for misfortunes, we would have arrived in the akhira completely destitute."

Sufyan Ibn 'Uyaynah, when commenting on the following ayah of the Quran: And We appointed leaders from among them who guided by Our command, so long as they persevered and firmly believed in Our signs. When they wanted to amputate Urwah Ibn Zubair's leg, they said to him, 'Shall we give you a drink so that you won't feel the pain?' He replied,' Allâh has given me this affliction in order to test my endurance shall I then act against His will?'

Urnar Ibn Abdal-Aziz said, "Whenever Allâh gives a blessing to a servant, and then takes it back from him, and the servant patiently endures his loss, then He rewards him with a blessing which is better than the one which He took back."

When Abu Bakr as-Siddiq, may Allâh be pleased with him, fell ill and people visited him, they said to him, "Shouldn't we call a doctor to see you?" He said, "The Doctor has already seen me." They said, "What did He say to you?" He said, "'Whatever I wish, I make it happen.'"

It has been related that Sa'id Ibn Jubair said, "Perseverance is the servant's acceptance before Allâh of the affliction that He has caused to befall him, his recognition that Allâh has taken it into account, and his hope that Allâh will reward him for It The servant may inwardly be in a state of fright and panic, but by exercising his self-control, nothing but perseverance can be observed in his demeanor."

Ibn Jubair's saying, "the servant's acceptance before Allâh of the affliction that He has caused to befall him", is like an explanation of the words, "Surely to Allâh we belong". Here, the servant accepts that he belongs to Allâh and that Allâh does as He wishes with His possessions.

His saying, "his hope that Allâh will reward him for it", is like an explanation of the words, "and surely to Him we are returning". It means that when we return to our Lord, He rewards us for our perseverance for the reward for perseverance is never lost.

"There are three things here: the correspondence of the remedy to the illness, the physician's dispensation of it, and reception by the ill person. If any of these is left out, healing is not attained, and when they all come together, the healing must occur, by the leave of God the Exalted."

— Ibn Qayyim al-Jawziyya

Chapter Fourteen
GRATITUDE

Gratitude is thanking the One who grants blessings for His generosity. The gratitude of a servant should have three qualities, without which it can hardly be considered to be gratitude. They are the inner recognition and appreciation of the blessing, speaking about it openly, and using it as a means to worshipping Him.

Gratitude is a matter for the heart, the tongue and the limbs. The heart is for knowledge and love of Him; the tongue is for thanking and praising Him; and the limbs are to be used in obeying the One Who is being thanked, and in holding back from committing disobedient acts.

Allâh, Glorious and Exalted is He, has linked gratitude with belief. He says that He does not need to punish His creatures if they thank Him and believe in Him. He says:

What has Allâh to do with punishing you, if you are grateful and you believe?

The Glorious and Mighty also says that the people who are grateful are singled out from the rest of His servants because of the mercy that He displays towards them.

The Mighty and Glorious says:

And thus We test some of them by means of others, so that they say, "Are these the ones whom Allâh has favored from amongst us?" Is not Allâh best Aware of those who give thanks?

He divides people into those who are grateful and those who are ungrateful; and the most displeasing thing to Him is ingratitude and its people; and the most precious thing to Him is gratitude and its people: Surely We have shown him the way, whether he is grateful or ungrateful.

And also: And when your Lord proclaimed: "If you are thankful I will give you more, but if you are ungrateful, then surely My punishment is terrible indeed."

In these Ayat, Allâh makes the granting of more blessings conditional on gratitude. There is no limit to the in- crease in His blessings, just as there is no limit to being grateful to Him. Allâh, Mighty and Glorious is He, has made a great deal of reward dependent on His will. He says: And if you fear poverty, Allâh will enrich you through His generosity, if He wills. Surely Allâh is Knowing, Wise.

And also: And He forgives whomever He wills.

And also: And Allâh turns in mercy towards whomever He wills.

He puts no limit on His reward for gratitude when He refers to it: We shall reward those who are thankful.

When the enemy of Allâh, shaytan, learned of the value of gratitude and that it is one of the most exalted and highest states he directed his efforts towards distancing people from it:

"Then will I approach them from in front of them and from behind them, and from their right and from their left; and You will find that most of them are not grateful."

Allâh has described the grateful ones among His worshippers as being few in number: And only a few of My servants are grateful.

The Prophet is reported to have stayed up in prayer all night until his feet swelled up. He was asked, "Why do you do this when Allâh has already forgiven you all your past and future wrong actions?" He, may Allâh bless him and grant him peace, said, "Should I not still be a grateful servant?"

The Prophet once told Mu'adh, "By Allâh, you are dear to me! So do not forget to say at the end of each prayer, "O Allâh, help me in remembering You, in being grateful to You and in serving You well." Gratitude is linked to Allâh's generosity and it is what makes it increase. Omar Ibn Abdal-Aziz said, "Join Allâh's generosity towards you to your gratitude towards Him."

Ibn Abi'd-Dunya reported that Ali Ibn Abi Talib, may Allâh be pleased with him, said to a man from the tribe of Hamazan, "Allâh's generosity is connected to gratitude, and gratitude is linked to increase in His generosity. The generosity of Allâh will not stop increasing unless the gratitude of His servant ceases."

Al-Hasan said, "Speak about His generosity frequently, for speaking about it is gratitude."

Allâh commanded His Messenger, may Allâh bless him and grant him peace, to speak of His Lord's generosity in the ayah:

And speak about the blessings of your Lord.

Allâh, Exalted is He, is pleased when the effect of His generosity on His servant is made apparent, for this in it-self is a form of gratitude that speaks for itself.

When Abu al-Mughirah used to be asked how he was, he would say, "We are immersed in the Lord's generosity, and incapable of being sufficiently grateful. He is most loving towards us, even though He does not need us, and we are disrespectful towards Him, even though we are utterly dependent on Him."

Sharih said, "Whenever a servant is afflicted with a misfortune, Allâh grants him three things: that it does not affect his faith; that it is not more severe than it might have been; and that, as it was decreed, it has already happened and is over."

Yunus Ibn Ubaid reported that Abu Ghunaimah was once asked, "How are you?" He replied, "I am caught be- tween two blessings whose nature is such that I do not know which of them is more excellent: my wrong actions which Allâh has concealed for me, so that no one can taunt me about them; or the affection for me which Allâh has placed in the hearts of His creatures, and which, because of my actions and deeds, I do not deserve."

Suffian said about this ayah of the Quran:

Leave Me (to deal) with those who reject these words. We shall gradually lead them on, in ways which they do not perceive, that Allâh makes His blessings pleasing to them, while withholding the ability to be grateful from them.

Others have said that whenever such people commit a sin, He confers a blessing on them.

A man once asked Abu Hazim, "O Abu Hazim, what is the gratitude of the eyes?" He replied, "It is to reveal whatever good they see and to veil whatever bad they see."

The man said, "And what is the gratitude of the ears?" He replied, "If you hear something good with them you understand it, and if you hear something bad you reject it."

The man asked, "And what is the gratitude of the hands?" He said, "Do not use them to take what is not yours, and do not restrain them from giving what is due to Allâh."

The man asked, "And what is the gratitude of the stomach?" He replied, "That its lower part is for food and its upper part is for knowledge," (i.e. it should not be stuffed full of food).

The man asked, "What is the gratitude of the private parts?" Abu Hazim replied by reciting the ayat of the Quran:

And those who guard their chastity, except with those to whom they are married, or the servants whom they own, for them there is no blame; but those whose de- sires exceed these limits are wrongdoers.

The man asked, "What is the gratitude of the feet?" He replied, "If you learn of the death of a righteous man who used to use his feet in doing good deeds and acts of worship, then use them in the same way as he did; whereas if the man who has died was someone despicable to you, then turn away from what he used to do and be grateful to Allâh.

"And as for the one who uses only his tongue to express his gratitude, he is like a man who only covers him-self with the hem of his garment without putting it on, so it is of no use to him in either the heat, or the cold, or the snow, or the rain."

A man of knowledge once wrote to his brother, "We have been granted so many of Allâh's blessings in spite of our many acts of disobedience that it is impossible for us to count them. We do not know which to be most grateful for the best of our good actions, which He enabled us to do, or the ugliest of our wrong actions which He has veiled for us."

"It is recorded in the two Sahihs that the Prophet, God grant him blessing and peace, said: "Shun the seven destroyers." They said, "What are they?" He said, "Ascribing partners to God, sorcery, killing a soul that God has forbidden except justly, consuming usury, consuming an orphan's property, fleeing from the battlefield, and slandering chaste, innocent believing women."

— Ibn Qayyim al-Jawziyy

Chapter Fifteen

COMPLETE RELIANCE ON ALLÂH

Complete reliance on Allâh is the sincere dependence of the heart on Allâh in the servant's endeavors in pursuing his interests and safeguarding himself against anything that may be harmful to his well-being both in this life and in the akhira. And for whoever fears Allâh, He prepares a way for- ward for him, and He provides for him from where he does not expect. And for whoever relies on Allâh, then He is enough for him.

A person who fears Allâh and relies completely on Him, will find that these two qualities are sufficient for him both in matter" of this world and of his deen.

Omar Ibn al-Khuttab, may Allâh be pleased with him, said, "I heard the Messenger of Allâh say, 'If you had all relied on Allâh as you should rely on Him, then He would have certainly provided for you as He provides for the birds, who wake up hungry in the morning and return with full stomachs at dusk.'"

Abu Hatim ar-Razi said that this hadith establishes the fundamental principle that reliance on Allâh is one of the most important means of acquiring one's sustenance and provision.

Sa'id Ibn jubair said, "Reliance on Allâh is an essential part of faith." Possessing the state of reliance, however, does not prevent you from utilizing the ways and means which Allâh has decreed for His creation. These are His laws, and He has commanded us to use ways and means, while at the same time He has instructed us to rely on Him. Endeavoring to make use of the ways and means in His Universe with our limbs is obedience, and relying on Him in our hearts is faith in Him. Allâh says: O you who believe, take your precautions.

Sahl said, "Whoever questions actions (e.g. striving to earn a living) questions the very validity of the Sunnah, and whoever questions reliance on Allâh questions faith itself."

Reliance is the state of the Prophet, while striving to earn a living is his Sunnah, and whoever behaves in accordance with the state of the Prophet must not abandon his Sunnah.

It has been said, "Ignoring ways and means is doubting the need for the shari'ah of Islam, while trusting entirely in ways and means is doubting the Reality of Tawhid (the existence of Allâh).

There are three kinds of actions that the servant has: First, the acts of obedience which Allâh has commanded His servants to do, since He has made them the means for rescuing them from the Fire and their entering the Garden. These must be done, while at the same time still relying on Allâh when doing them and seeking this outcome for there is no strength and no power except from Him.

Whatever He, the Exalted, wishes to be has already happened, and whatever He wishes not to be will never happen.

Whoever does not fulfil one of the duties which have been imposed on him by Allâh deserves to be punished in this life and in the next life in accordance with the shari'ah and as decreed by Allâh, the Exalted.

Yusul Ibn Asbat said, "Do what you do like a man who can only be saved by his actions, and rely completely on Allâh like a man who can only be afflicted by the afflictions that have already been decreed for him."

Second, the actions which Allâh has made a part of life in this world, and in which He has told His servants to take part such as eating when hungry, drinking when thirsty, seeking shade in the heat, keeping warm in cold weather, and other such things, Being involved in such actions is also a duty, Whoever does not do so, to the extent that he does himself harm by abandoning them even though he was perfectly capable of doing them has been negligent and deserves punishment.

Third, the actions which Allâh has made a part of life in general, without their being essential Allâh can make exceptions for whomever of His servants He chooses.

There are several kinds of these actions, one of which is taking medicine. The ulama' have given varying answers to the following question: Is it better for a sick person to take medicine or, in the case of those who rely completely on Allâh, to abstain from taking it?

There are two better known answers to this question: Imam Ahmad says that reliance on Allâh for the one who has it is better. The Imam cites the saying of the Prophet, "Seventy thousand people of my Ummah will enter the Garden without being taken to account or being punished, They are the ones who do not make talismans, or seek them, or look for omens, or treat their body by burning, and who completely rely on their Lord:' Those ulama' who approve of taking medicine, say that the Prophet used to take it, and he only did what was best; and that the above hadith only applies to the use of ta-lismans, which are rightly regarded with suspicion because they can lead to reliance on other than Allâh, and which are accordingly equated with looking for omens and treatment by burning.

Mujahid, 'Ikrimah, an-Nukha'i and several of our predecessors said, "No one has been given permission to totally abandon trying to use the ways and means of this world for treating his afflictions, except one whose heart has altogether ceased to relate to the creation."

Ishaq Ibn Rahawayh was asked, "Can a man engage in warfare without making any preparation for it?" He answered, "He can, and if he is like Abdullah Ibn jubair otherwise he cannot."

"Part of [the benefit of God's making one fall into sin] is also that the servant attains the ranks of humility, meekness and lowliness as well as neediness before Him, for the ego has a tendency to rival lordship; if it had the power it would claim what the Pharaoh claimed, but He has predestined and dominated and all other than Him is incapable and dominated."

— Ibn Qayyim al-Jawziyy

Chapter Sixteen

LOVE OF ALLÂH

Loving Allâh, the Glorious, the Exalted, is the ultimate aim of all stations, and the summit of all states. Having attained the state of true love for Allâh, each station that follows it is one of its fruits and a branch from its roots such as longing, intimacy and contentment. Each station that precedes it is a step towards it such as repentance, perseverance and doing without, or zuhud.

The most beneficial, the most sincere, the most elevated and the most exalted kind of love is most certainly the love of the One Whom hearts were created to love, and for Whom creation was brought into existence to adore. Allâh is the One to Whom hearts turn in love, exaltation, glorification, humility, submission and worship. Such worship cannot be directed towards other than Him. It is the perfection of love accompanied by complete submission and humility. Allâh, the Exalted, is loved for His own sake in every respect. All except Him are loved for the love they give m return. All the revealed Books, and the messages of all the Prophets, bear witness to the love that is due to- wards Him, as does the natural impulse He has created in all His servants, the intellect He has given them, and the blessings He has poured on them.

Hearts, as they mature, come to love whomever is merciful and kind towards them. So how much greater is their love for Him from Whom all kindness springs!

Every good thing enjoyed by His creation is one of His limitless blessings, and He is One, with no associates and no partners. And whatever good you have it is from Allâh; and then, when misfortune comes to you, you cry to Him for help,

And also: And from among mankind there are some who take for themselves (Objects of worship as) rivals to Allâh, loving them as they should (only) love Allâh, And those who believe are stronger in their love for Allâh.

And also: O you who believe, whoever of you becomes a rebel against his deen, (know that in his place) Allâh will bring a people whom He loves and who love Him, humble towards the believers, harsh towards the disbelievers, fighting in the way of Allâh, and not fearing the blame of anyone who blames.

The Prophet: has sworn that no servant truly believes until he, may Allâh bless him and grant him peace, is dearer to that servant than his own child, father, and all of mankind.

The Prophet: also said to Omar Ibn ai-Khuttab, may Allâh be pleased with him, "even until I am dearer to you than your own self:' This means that you are not a true believer until your love for the Prophet: reaches this level. If the Prophet: must take precedence over our ownselves when it comes to what we love and what this entails, then is not Allâh, Exalted is He, even more deserving of our love and adoration than our own selves?

Everything that comes from Him to His servants, whether it is something that they love or something that they hate, directs us to love of Him. His giving and His withholding, the good fortune and the misfortune that He decrees for His servants and His abasing them and elevating them, His justice and His grace, His giving life and taking it away again, His compassion, generosity and veiling of His servants' wrong actions, His forgiveness and patience, His response to His servants' supplications even though He is not in any need of His servants whatsoever all this invites hearts to worship Him and love Him.

If a human being were to do the smallest amount of any of these things to another, that person would not be able to restrain his heart from loving hm. How can a servant not love, with all his heart and body, the One Who is constantly Merciful and Generous towards him in spite of all his wrong actions?

Allâh's mercy descends upon His servant from the heavens, while the servant's wrong actions rise up to him from the earth. Allâh seeks His servant's friendship and love by means of His generosity towards him, even though He is not in any need of him. The servant, on the other hand, invites Allâh's anger through his disobedience and wrong actions, even though he is in need of His assistance.

Neither Allâh's mercy nor His generosity towards the servant deter him from disobeying his Lord. In the same way, neither the servant's disobedience nor his wrong actions deter Allâh ta"Aia from granting him His blessings.

Furthermore, while anyone whom we love and who loves us may behave like this for personal gain, Allâh, Mighty and Glorious is He, does so in order to benefit us.

Furthermore, while anyone with whom we trade will not do business with us if he does not expect to make a profit from the transaction and he will do what he can to make a profit one way or another Allâh, Mighty and Glorious is He, trades with us in order to enable us to make the best and greatest profit for ourselves from our transaction with Hm. Thus one good deed counts as between ten and seven hundred good deeds, or even more, while a bad deed is recorded as only one bad deed and can be swiftly wiped out.

Furthermore, He, Glorious is He, created us for Himself and He created everything for us, both in this world and in the next. Who else, then, deserves to be loved and pleased more than Allâh ta'Ala?

Furthermore, all that we and the whole creation, for that matter require and need is with Him. He is the Most Generous. He gives His servants more than they need, even before they ask him. He is pleased with even a little right action and increases its rewards. He forgives untold wrong actions and wipes them out. Whatever is in the heavens and the earth supplicates to Him. Every day He is on a new affair. The multiplicity of things never bewilder Him, nor is He ever made weary by the insistent pleas of His servants. Indeed He is pleased with those who persist in their supplication.

He is pleased with those of His servants who seek His assistance, and He is angry with those who do not. He is displeased when He sees a servant being disobedient and not caring about his actions, and yet He veils His servant's wrong actions while the servant himself does not veil them. He has mercy on His servant while the servant does not have mercy on himself.

He has called him to His acceptance and mercy through His compassion and generosity, but he declines. He has sent messengers to him and made His covenant known through them. He, Glorious is He, even draws near him and says, "Is there anyone who is calling on Me, so that I may answer his prayer? Is there anyone who is seeking My forgiveness, so that I may forgive him?"

How, then, can hearts not love Him, the One Who and no one other than Him grants rewards, answers prayers, pardons mistakes, forgives sins, veils wrong actions, dispels grief and drives away sorrow?

He alone, Exalted is He, is worthy of remembrance, gratitude, worship and praise. He is the most generous to be asked, the most liberal to give, the most merciful to par- don, the mightiest to assist and the most dependable to rely on. He is more merciful to His servant than a mother is to her baby. He is also more pleased by the repentance of the penitent sinner than a man who is overjoyed to find his riding beast with all his provisions still on its back after he had lost it in a barren land and had given up all hope of survival.

He is the King, with no partner, the One, the Unique, Who has no equal. Everything will perish except His Face. He is not obeyed unless it is by His command, nor is He disobeyed without His knowing it. He is pleased with the obedient servant for his obedience, even though it could not have occurred without His help and assistance. He pardons and forgives even after He has been disobeyed. And yet the rights which are due to Him are the ones which are most rejected and neglected.

He is the nearest witness, the most sublime protector, the most true to His Word, and the most just of all judges.

He knows the secrets of the selves. There is not an animal of whose forelock He does not have a hold. . He records the actions and decides the lifetimes of His slaves. To Him the secrets in the hearts are known and the Unseen is revealed. Everyone yearns for Him, faces humble themselves before the Light of His Face, and minds are completely incapable of understanding the Essence of His Being. All the evidence that confronts the heart and mind bears witness to the impossibility of there being anything like Him. By the Light of His Face every form of darkness has been enlightened, the heavens and the earth have been illuminated, and the whole creation has been set in order. He does not sleep, nor is it fitting for Him to do so. The ac-tion of the night are presented before Him before day- break, and those of the day before nightfall. He is veiled by pure light, and if the veil were to be removed, then the radiance of His Light would engulf all of His creation that His vision contains.

Love of Allâh the Almighty gives life to the heart and sustains the soul. The heart experiences no pleasure, nor feels any joy, nor tastes any success not even life if it does not have this love. If the heart loses this love, then the loss it suffers is more severe than that of the eye when it is deprived of its sight and the ear when it is deprived of its hearing.

Even worse than this, the decay of the heart when it is devoid of love for its Creator, Source, and True God, is far worse than that of the body when it no longer contains the soul. This truth is only recognized by the people who are alive, for a wound does not pain the dead.

Fath al-Ma Wsili said, "The lover finds no other pleasure in life and does not neglect remembering Allâh for an instant."

A righteous man once said, "The lover is always With Him: he remembers Him continually and constantly with longing, using every possible means and nawafil to please Him."

Another man said in a poem: And love your Lord by serving Him,

For lovers are but servants of the Beloved.

When she was giving counsel to her children, one of the women of the Salaf once said to them, "Make it a habit to love and obey Allâh, for those who have taqwa take their obedience to the point where their body experiences aversion for anything other than obedience.

If the cursed one (shaytan) tries to tempt them to do something wrong, the wrong action is ashamed and avoids them because of the way in which it is rejected by them."

Abdullah Ibn al-Mubarak recited: You disobey Allâh, and yet you still claim to love Him. By Allâh, such behavior is disgusting, by any standard.'

You would have obeyed Him had your love been true, for the lover is always obedient to the Beloved.

"Forsaking action for the sake of other people is to seek their admiration. To act for the sake of their admiration is to associate others with Allah. Devotion is when Allah frees you from both of these states."

— Ibn Qayyim al-Jawziyya

Chapter Seventeen

CONTENTMENT WITH THE DECREE OF ALLÂH

The servant may experience one of two states as regards what he dislikes: the state of being content, or that of being patient. Being content is a praiseworthy quality, while being patient is a duty which the believer must fulfil.

At some times, the people of contentment witness the Wisdom and Beauty of the One Who Tests when He tests His servant, and they see that He is always Right in what- ever He decrees.

At other times, they witness the Might and Majesty and Perfection of the One Who Tests, to such an extent that they become completely immersed in these Attributes of Allâh, Exalted is He, so that they do not experience any pain.

This station can only be attained by those who have great knowledge and love. And so it is possible that they find pleasure in whatever they have been afflicted with- because it has come to them from their Beloved.

The Difference between Contentment and Patience

Being patient involves restraining the self and preventing it from giving in to resentment, in spite of any suffering that it experiences in the hope that the misfortune which afflicts it will come to an end as well as restraining the limbs from behaving badly, out of impatience.

Being content, on the other hand, involves feeling at ease in accepting the Divine Decree, and being unconcerned with when any suffering will stop, even though it is being experienced. Being content alleviates any suffering by reason of the heart's immersion in the spirit of certainty and knowledge. If the contentment increases in its intensity, then it removes the experiencing of any suffering altogether.

It has been related on the authority of Anas Ibn Malik that the Prophet: said, "When Allâh loves someone then He tests him: as for whoever is content Allâh will be pleased with him; and as for whoever is discontented.

Allâh will be displeased with him." 'Ibn Mas'ud, may Allâh be pleased with him, said, "Allâh the Almighty has, in His justice and Wisdom, placed refreshment and joy in certainty and contentment, and He has placed sadness and sorrow in doubt and discontentment."

When commenting on the ayah, *No misfortune happens without the permission of Allâh and as for whoever believes in Allâh, He guides his heart; and Allâh knows all things*,

'Alqama said, "This concerns the misfortune which afflicts the servant: he knows that it has come from Allâh, and so he comes to terms with it and feels content with it."

As regards the ayah, *whoever acts righteously, whether male or female, and is a believer, We will surely give him life with a good life, and We will surely give them their reward in accordance with the best of what they used to do.*

Abu Mu'awiyya al-Aswar said, "'A good life' means being satisfied and content."

Ali Ibn Abi Talib, may Allâh be pleased with him, once saw 'Adiyy Ibn Hatim looking sorrowful and so he asked him, "Why are you so sad, O 'Adiyy?" 'Adiyy replied, "How can I not be in such a state, when both of my sons have been killed a J my eye gouged out?" So Ali said to him, "O 'Adiyy, whoever is content with the Decree of Allâh will surely experience it and be rewarded for it; and whoever is not content with the Decree of Allâh will surely experience it and Allâh will make his actions worthless."

Abu'd-Darda' visited a man on his death-bed and found him praising Allâh, so he said to him, "You are right! Allâh, Mighty and Glorious is He, likes us to be con- tent with whatever He decrees."

Al-Hasan al-Basri said, "Whoever is content with what he has, Allâh will make it enough for him and give it blessing; and whoever is not content, Allâh will neither make it enough for him nor give it blessing."

Omar Ibn Abdal-Aziz said, "I have nothing that gives me any joy, except when what has been decreed by Allâh happens." He was once asked, "What do you desire?" He replied, "Whatever Allâh, Mighty and Glorious is He, decrees."

Abdal-Wahid Ibn Zaid said, "Being content is the greatest door to Allâh, the Garden of this life, and a place of rest for the worshippers."

It has also been said, "There will be no station in the akhira better than that of those who are content with whatever Allâh decrees, at all times. Whoever enjoys the quality of contentment will be raised to the best of stations."

On discovering one morning that he had lost a great many camels, an Arab of the desert said, "By Him of Whom I am one of His slaves, were it not for some envious and malicious enemies, I would not have been pleased to see my camels still alive and in their pen and something which Allâh had decreed not taking place."

"Imam Ahmad said: "Allah, the Exalted, has mentioned patience in 90 places in the Quran."

— Ibn Qayyim al-Jawziyya

Chapter Eighteen

HOPE IN ALLÂH

This is the peaceful state of a heart that awaits what is dear to it. If the means by which what the heart awaits may come are not present, then stupidity and folly would be more accurate descriptions of its state. If, on the other hand, what it awaits is certain to happen, then neither can certain hope be the term to use in describing its state: one cannot say, "I wish the sun would rise at sunrise", but one can say, "I wish it would rain".

Those who study the heart have taught that this world is like land which is cultivated for its fruits in the next world: that the heart is like the earth, that belief is like the seeds, and that acts of obedience are like ploughing up the soil and clearing it for planting and digging channels to bring water to it.

The heart which is in love with this world is like barren earth in which seeds cannot sprout. The Day of Resurrection is like the day of the harvest, and no one reaps what he did not sow. No seed other than the seed of belief can grow, and belief rarely brings forth any fruit if the heart is rotten and lacking morality.

In the same way that seeds do not sprout in barren earth, so a servant's hope for Allâh's forgiveness can be compared to the hope of a farmer: If anyone searches for fertile soil, sows it with good healthy seeds, supplies it with what it needs when it needs it, pulls out the weeds and anything else that might hinder or ruin the growth of the crop, and then sits waiting for Allâh's blessings in the form of His keeping unfavorable weather and destructive pests away until the crop has finished growing and is ripe then his waiting can be described as hope.

If, however, he sows the seeds in hard, barren soil which is too high up for water to reach it, and does nothing to care for the seedlings, and then sits waiting for a harvest then his waiting can only be described as folly and stupidity, not hope.

So, the term hope only applies to waiting with longing and yearning for something to happen, after all the means which will assist in the realization of this desire that is, all those means which are within the servant's power and choice have been utilized.

The things which are not within the servant's control, and which are entirely within the domain of Allâh's generosity, also play a part. Allâh, Exalted is He, is able to pre- vent all harmful phenomena and obstacles, if He so wishes.

If the servant sows the seeds of belief, and waters them with obedience to and worship of Allâh, and purifies his heart of bad elements, and then waits for Allâh's blessings in the form of His keeping him steady in that state until his death, and then granting him an excellent end and His forgiveness then his waiting is truly hoping for the best.

Allâh, the Exalted, says: Surely those who believe and those who make him and struggle in the way of Allâh, these are the ones who have hope of the mercy of Allâh; and Allâh is Forgiving, Compassionate.

This means that such people are worthy of hoping for Allâh's mercy. Allâh did not intend to restrict hope in Him to them alone, for others can also have hope, but He distinguishes them as the only people whose hope is really well founded.

The one whose hope guides him to obedience of Allâh and deters him from rebelling against Him has true hope; whereas the hope which leads a person on to idleness and being immersed in wrong actions is only stupidity in disguise.

It should be pointed out that anyone who hopes for something must satisfy three conditions: First, he should hold dear what he hopes for. Second, he should be afraid of missing it.

Third, he should strive to achieve what he hopes for. If hope is not connected to any one of these prerequisites, then it is only wishful thinking hope is a different matter altogether.

Everyone who is hopeful is fearful. Whoever walks a path, makes haste when he fears that he may miss the goal that he hopes for.

It has been related by Abu Huraira that the Prophet, may Allâh bless him and grant him peace, said, "Whoever is afraid of being plundered by the enemy sets out in the early part of the night, and whoever sets out early reaches his goal. Be on your guard! The treasures of Allâh are dear and precious. Wake up! The treasure of Allâh is the Garden."! Allâh, Glorious and Exalted is He, says:

Say: "O My servants who have wronged their souls, do not despair of the mercy of Allâh, for surely Allâh forgives all sins; surely He is Forgiving, Compassionate.

And also: And surely your Lord is full of forgiveness for man- kind for their wrongdoing.

Omar Ibn Abdal-Aziz reported on the authority of his father, may Allâh be pleased with both of them that the Prophet said, "Whenever a Muslim dies, and Allâh casts a Jew or a Christian into the Fire in his place."

It has been transmitted on the authority of Omar Ibn al-Khuttab, may Allâh be pleased with him, that some prisoners were brought before the Messenger of Allâh - amongst them there was a woman who was searching for someone in the crowd. When he found a baby amongst the prisoners, she took it in her arms, cradled it next to her breast, and allowed it to suckle.

Then the Messenger of Allâh said, "Do you think this woman would ever throw her child into the Fire?" We said, "By Allâh, as long as it was in her power, she would never throw her child into the Fire!"

Then the Messenger of Allâh said, "Allâh is more merciful to His servants than this woman is to her child." It has been related on the authority of Abu Huraira that he heard the Messenger of Allâh: say, "When Allâh created the creation, He decreed something for Himself, and a clear record is with Him confirming that, 'Truly, My mercy prevails over My wrath."

It has been reported on the authority of Anas that he heard the Messenger of Allâh say, "Allâh, Exalted is He, has said, 'O son of Adam, as long as you call on Me and ask of Me, I will forgive you for what you have done, and I shall not mind. O son of Adam, were your sins to reach the clouds of the sky and were you then to ask forgiveness of Me, I would forgive you. O son of Adam, were you to come to Me with sins nearly as great as the earth, and were you then to face Me without having associated anything with Me, I would bring you forgiveness nearly as great as it.'"

Yahya Ibn Mu'adh said, "In my opinion, the worst kind of self-delusion is for someone to sin excessively and then to hope for forgiveness without feeling any remorse; or it is to expect to draw near to Allâh, the Exalted, without obeying or worshipping Him; or it is to hope for the fruit of the Garden after having only planted the seeds for the Fire; or it is to seek the abode of the obedient through com- mitting wrong actions; or it is to expect a reward after having done nothing worthwhile; or it is to place hope in Allâh, Glorious and Mighty is He, after having exceeded all the limits."

If a heart becomes attached to anything other than Allah, Allah makes him dependent on what he is attached to. And he will be betrayed by it.

Ibn Qayyim Al-Jawziyya

Chapter Nineteen

FEAR OF ALLÂH

Fear is the spur with which Allâh urges His servants to-wards knowledge and action so that they can draw nearer to Him. It is the pain and anguish of the heart when it senses that harm is imminent. Fear is what restrains the body from being disobedient and compels it to worship and service. When fear is lacking, this leads to negligence and boldness in committing sins, whereas too much fear results in a state of hopelessness and despair.

Fear of Allâh, Exalted is He, sometimes springs from knowledge of Him, and of His Attributes the knowledge that it would be of little concern to Him to obliterate the heavens and the earth, and that nothing can stop Him from doing so if He so wishes.

At other times it is caused by the enormity of the wrong actions which the servant commits.

At other times it is caused by a combination of all these things: the degree of a servant's fear depends on his awareness of his own faults, and on his awareness of Allâh's Glory, Might and Self-Sufficiency and of the fact that He is not accountable for what He does, while His servants are.

The person who fears His Lord most is the one who has most knowledge of Him and of himself. This is why the Prophet, peace and blessings be upon him, said, "By Allâh, of all people, I am the one with the most knowledge of Allâh, and I fear Him the most."

Imam ash-Sha'bi was once addressed as, "O knowledge- able one." He replied, "I am not for the knowledgeable one is the one who fears Allâh, as He, Mighty and Glorious is He, says: Surely those of His servants who know fear Allâh.

Those Who Fear Allâh

The one who experiences fear is not the one who weeps and wipes his eyes, but the one who abandons whatever may bring punishment upon him. Dhu'n-Nun al-Misri was once asked, "When is a servant really afraid?" He replied, "When he is in the same state as a sick man who seeks protection in Allâh out of fear that his sickness will be prolonged."

Abu'l-Qassim al-Hakeem said, "Whoever fears something runs away from it, while whoever fears Allâh runs towards Him." Al-Fudayl Ibn 'Iyyad said, "If you are asked whether you fear Allâh, do not reply; for if you say 'Yes', you would be lying, and if you say 'No', it would mean that you do not believe in Him."

Fear burns up forbidden desires, and the wrong actions which can be so dear to a servant soon become distasteful, just as honey becomes repugnant to someone who desires it, if he discovers that it is poisoned. Fear tames the limbs and fills the heart with submission, humility and tranquility. Arrogance, hatred and envy depart from it, and it is filled with Him, through fear of Him and through contemplating the danger of His punishment and so it becomes occupied with nothing other than Him, and has no concern other than contemplation, bringing itself to account and striving in the way of Allâh.

A servant with such a heart becomes watchful over every breath and every moment, and constantly reprimands the self for its inner thoughts, its actions and its words. His state is like that of a person who is trapped in the claws of a lion, not knowing whether it will leave him alone and allow him to escape, or whether it will attack him and kill him. Thus he becomes both inwardly and outwardly occupied with what he fears. There is no room in him for anything other than what he fears. This is the state of a person who is overwhelmed by fear of Allâh.

The Merits of Fear of Allâh

Allâh, Mighty and Glorious is He, grants guidance, mercy, knowledge and acceptance to those who fear Him. Guidance and mercy for those who fear their Lord. And also: Surely those of His servants who know fear Allâh. And also: Their reward is with their Lord: Gardens of Eden underneath which rivers flow wherein they will dwell forever; Allâh is pleased with them, and they are pleased with Him; this is for whoever fears his Lord.

Allâh has commanded His servants to fear Him and has made belief conditional upon fear. He, Glorious and Mighty is He, says: Fear Me if you are believers.

This is why it is inconceivable that a believer can be de- void of fear of Allâh, however slight it may be. The weakness of his fear is in proportion to the weakness of his knowledge and faith.

The Prophet said, "No believer who has wept from fear of Allâh, Exalted is He, will ever enter the Fire unless milk returns back into its udder."

Al-Fudayl Ibn 'Iyyad said, "Whoever fears Allâh will be guided by this fear to all good."

Ash-Shibli said, "There was never a time that I feared Allâh without my finding a door of wisdom and guidance opening up to Him." Yahya Ibn Mu'adh said, "Any wrong action committed by a believer is followed by two consequences: fear of punishment and hope for forgiveness." Allâh, the Exalted, says in the Quran:

Surely those who live in awe out of fear of their Lord, and those who believe in the signs of their Lord, and those who do not associate partners with their Lord in their worship, and those who give what they give with fear in their hearts because they are returning to their Lord it is these who hasten to do good, and in this they are foremost.

It has been reported by Aisha, may Allâh be pleased with her, that she said, ' asked the Messenger of Allâh about these ayat, saying, 'Are they those who drink intoxicants, and commit adultery and steal?' He, May Allâh bless him and grant him peace, said, 'No, O daughter of as-Sideeq, it is those who regularly fast and pray and give zakat and fear that their good deeds may not be accepted, it is these who hasten to do good.'"

It has been related on the authority of Abu Dharr, may Allâh be pleased with him, that the Messenger of Allâh recited the surah from the Quran beginning with the ayah: Has there ever been any period of time for man in which he was something not remembered?

Then he said, "I see what you do not see and I hear what you do not hear. Heaven has groaned and it has a right to groan. By Him in Whose hand my soul is, there is not a space of even four fingers width in which there is not an angel who prostrates his forehead before Allâh. I swear by Allâh that if you knew what I know, you would laugh little and weep much, and you would not take delight in women, but you would go out to an open space and call on Allâh for help. I wish I were a tree that could be cut down and cease to exist."

This hadith indicates that if we knew as much as the Prophet knew about the Might of Allâh, and His retribution for whoever disobeys Him, then our weeping and grief and fear for what might await us would be long lasting. We might never laugh at all.

Aisha, may Allâh be pleased with her, reported that whenever the wind changed and storms blew, the Prophet's demeanor would change and he would walk to and fro in the room in agitation, going out and then coming back in again. All of this was out of fear of Allâh's punishment.

Abdullah Ibn ash-Shukhair related that whenever the Messenger of Allâh started doing the prayer, a sound like a bubbling cauldron could be heard coming from his chest.

If you consider the state of the companions of the Holy Prophet, and the righteous men of this Ummah who succeeded them, may Allâh be pleased with all of them, you will find that they were fully involved in doing the best of deeds while, at the same time, they were full of fear of Allâh. We, on the other hand, all do things which fall far short of this example, and yet feel quite secure.

Abu Bakr as-Siddiq, may Allâh be pleased with him, said, "I wish I were no more than a hair on the side of a believing servant." Whenever he got up to do the prayer, he would be trembling like a leaf out of fear of Allâh.

Omar Ibn al-Khuttab, may Allâh be pleased with him, was once reading Sural atTur and when he came to the ayah: Surely the doom of your Lord will indeed come to pass. And he wept so intensely that he fell ill, so that people came to see how he was.

When he was on his death bed he told his son, "Put my cheek next to the earth so that Allâh may forgive me." Then he said, "I am doomed if He does not forgive me." He repeated the same words three times and then he died.

When he used to recite the Quran at night and read an ayah that filled him with fear, he would stay indoors for days on end so that people would come to visit him, thinking that he was ill. His frequent weeping etched two dark lines on his face.

Ibn Abbas once told him, "Allâh has brought many countries into the Muslim Ummah through you, and through you many a victory has been won." Omar replied, "All I hope for is to be saved. I desire neither reward nor punishment."

Uthman Ibn Affan, may Allâh be pleased with him, used to cry until his beard was soaked each time that he stood at a grave. He used to say, "If I were standing be- tween the Garden and the Fire, not knowing in which one of the two I would end up, I would rather be turned into ashes before !learned of my fate."

Abu'd-Darda' used to say, "If you knew what you will encounter after your death, you would never eat with any appetite, nor drink thirstily, nor enter houses to shelter, but you would go out into open spaces and beat your breast and weep at your lot. I wish I were a tree to be cut up and destroyed."

Ibn Abbas had skin under his eyes which looked like worn out sandal leather, due to his frequent weeping.

Ali Ibn Abi Tahb, may Allâh honor him, was once overwhelmed with sadness after completing the dawn prayer; he said, "Never before did I see anything like the companions of the Messenger of Allâh. Their hair was disheveled, their faces were pale, they were covered in dust, and the space between their eyes looked like the knees of goats. They had spent the night in prayer and recitation of the Quran, either on their feet or in prostration.

When the dawn came, they would spend it in remembrance of Allâh, swaying like trees on a stormy day, with tears streaming from their eyes until their clothes were soaked. By Allâh, it seems to me that the people who are around me now have passed the night fast asleep." Then he got up and was never seen laughing again, until he was stabbed to death by Ibn Muslim.

Musa Ibn Mas'ud said, "Whenever we sat in the company of Suffian, we would feel as if the Fire had surrounded us because of the fear and panic we could see in his eyes." Al-Hasan was once described as follows: "When- ever he approached us, it would seem as if he had only just returned from the burial of his best friend; whenever he sat in a company, he would be like a prisoner who has just been sentenced to death by having his head cut off, and whenever the Fire was mentioned, it would be as if it had been created especially for him."

It has been related that Zurarah Ibn Abu Awfa led some people in the dawn prayer and recited Sural al-Mudathir from the Quran. When he reached the words:

For when the trumpet shall sound, that will be- that Daya Day of Distress, he gasped and fell down dead.

Abdullah Ibn Amr Ibn al-As is reported to have said, "Weep, and if you cannot weep, then pretend to weep! I swear by Him in Whose hand my life is that if any of you really knew, you would plead until your voice went, and pray until your back was broken."

Happiness is attained by three things: being patient when tested, being thankful when receiving a blessing, and being repentant upon sinning.

Ibn Qayyim Al-Jawziyya

Chapter Twenty

THE LIFE OF THIS WORLD

The disapproval of this world that appears in the Book and the Hadith is not directed at its time aspect which is the alternation of night and day until the Day of Judgment. Allâh, the Mighty and Glorious, has provided them so that people who wish to do so can invoke His Name and be thankful during them.

It was once said, "The night and the day are like two treasure-chests, so be careful of what you do in them." Mujahid said, "Not a day passes which does not say, 'O son of Adam, I have come to you today and I will never come again, so be careful of what you do during my stay.' When the day has passed, it is folded up and sealed, never to be reopened by anyone until Allâh reopens it on the Day of Judgment." There is a poem that goes:

Life is nothing other than a road that leads to the Garden, or to the Fire. Its nights are a man's workshop, and its days are his market place. So time is the servant's capital. The Prophet said, "Whoever says, 'Exalted is Allâh and His are the Blessings', will have a palm tree planted for him in the Garden."

Consider how many palm trees a time waster misses the opportunity of planting.

The disapproval of this world that appears in the Book and the Hadith is not directed at its space aspect either, which is the earth and all its mountains, and seas, and rivers, and the treasures within it. All these are Allâh's blessings for His servants, so that they can make use of them, and contemplate them and thereby recognize the Oneness and Greatness of their Maker, Exalted is He. The disapproval is directed at the actions of the sons of Adam in this world, most of which do not have any good consequences; for as the Glorious and Exalted says: Know that the life of this world is only playing about and idle talk and showing off and boasting amongst yourselves, and competing in wealth and children. It is like a crop after rain whose growth pleases the farmer- but then it dries up, and you see it turn yellow, and then it becomes straw.

In this life, the sons of Adam' are divided into two types: The first type denies the existence of an abode which awaits Allâh's servants after this life is over, where reward and punishment are experienced. These are the ones about whom Allâh says: Surely those who do not look forward to their meeting with us, but are pleased with the life of this world and feel secure in it, and those who do not pay attention to Our signs their abode will be the Fire, because of what they used to earn.

Such people have only one concern, which is to enjoy life and pursue the pleasures and the Exalted says: And those who reject take it easy and eat like cattle eat and the Fire will be their abode.

The second type are those who accept that there is an abode after death, where there is both reward and punishment. These are the ones who follow the Messengers.

They fall into three categories: those who are unjust to themselves, those who are mean to themselves, and those who are swift in doing good deeds, by the will of Allâh.

First, those who are unjust to themselves form the majority. Most of them are content with the blossoms of this life and its pleasures, helping themselves to them and using them in ways which Allâh has not commanded. The world appears to them to be their greatest concern, and with it they are satisfied; they only love and hate for its sake.

These are the people who play about and chatter and are diverted by the attractions of this world. Although they may believe in the akhira in a general way, they have not discovered what this life is meant for, nor are they aware that it is only a stopping place where provisions for the final journey can be acquired.

Second, those who are mean to themselves are those who take what is permitted from this world and fulfil their duties in it, but who then pursue what lies beyond these duties for the sake of their own pleasure and in order to enjoy the delights of this world.

Such people will not be punished for doing so, but their pleasure seeking will result in their rank being diminished. Omar Ibn Al-Khuttab, may Allâh be pleased with him, said, "If it had not been for the "fact that my station in the Garden might be diminished, I would have imitated you in your life of ease; but Allâh has warned some people by saying: You squandered the good things that you had in the life of the world, and you sought contentment in them."

Third, those who are swift in doing good deeds are the ones who understand what this world is meant for, and they act accordingly. They know that Allâh has only put His servants in this world in order to see which of them have the best actions. Surely We have put what is on the earth as a glittering show so that We may test them, as to which of them have the best actions.

This means that Allâh has put what is on the earth in order to test us, to see who is going to avoid the pleasures of this world and look for success in the next world, for: And surely We shall turn what is on it into a heap of dust.

Those who race to do good deeds only take from this world whatever provisions are necessary for the journey. The Messenger of Allâh said, "What have I to do with this world? As regards this world, I am like a rider who rests under the shade of a tree, and then continues his journey and leaves it."

The Prophet, peace and blessings be upon him, also told Ibn Omar, "Be in this life as if you were a stranger or a wayfarer."

Whenever the intention behind taking pleasure in what is halal is the obedience and worship of Allâh, then the enjoyment of such pleasures is regarded as an act of obedience for which the servant is rewarded.

As Mu'adh Ibn Jabal, may Allâh be pleased with him, said, "look forward to Allâh's reward for the time which spend asleep, just as I look forward to it for the time which I spend awake.'"

Sa'id Ibn Jubair said, "The provisions of arrogance and pride are what distract you from the akhira. The provisions that do not distract you are the ones which you need in order to reach what is better than the provisions them-selves."

Yahya Ibn Mu'adh said, "How can I not love this world in which I have been blessed with sustenance that gives me life, when use this life for worship by means of which I can earn the reward of the Garden?"

Abu Safwan ar-Ra'ini was once asked, "What is the life of this world which is criticized in the Quran, and which those who are prudent should avoid?" He replied, "Everything that you do in this world with the intention of making a profit in this world is blameworthy, and everything that you do in order to profit in the next world has nothing to do with this world."

Al-Hasan said, "How sweet and good the life of this world is for the mumin -for without having to make too much effort, he takes his provision from it for the Garden; and how awful the life of this world is for the kafir and the munafiq for they waste their nights and they take their provision from it for the Fire!"

Abu Musa related that the Prophet said, "Whoever is in love with his life in this world damages his life in the next world, and whoever is in love with his life in the next world damages his life in this world and you should prefer what lasts forever to what is destined to vanish."

Awn Ibn Abdullah said, "This life and the next life hang in the balance in the heart as if on scales. Whichever one predominates, the other becomes lighter and less significant." Wahab said, "This life and the next life are like a man with two wives. If he pleases one he incurs the wrath of the other."

Abu'd-Darda said, "If you swear to me that a certain man is the most God-fearing amongst you, I will swear to you that he is the best amongst you."

Abdullah Ibn Mas'ud addressed some people saying, "You have undertaken more good actions than the companions of the Messenger of Allâh ever did, but they are still better than you are because they turned away from worldly pleasures and gains."

The Harm in Love for this World

Imam Ahmad wrote, on the authority of Suffian, that Jesus the son of Mary, peace be on them, used to say, "Love for this world is the root of all evil, and having money is a serious illness." He was asked, "What ill effects does it have?" He replied, "Whoever has it is never safe from pride and self-delusion."

They said, "What if someone is safe from these defects?" He said, "His being preoccupied with doing well will distract him from the remembrance of Allâh, Glorious and Mighty is He."

Love for this world is what fills the Fire, while doing without the pleasures of this world is what fills the Garden. Being intoxicated with love for this world is more disastrous than being intoxicated by alcohol, because a person who is drunk with this world only finally comes to his senses in the darkness of his grave.

Yahya Ibn Muadh said, "The life of this world is the wine of shaytan, and whoever is intoxicated by it only wakes up once he is amongst the hordes of the dead, lamenting among the losers."

The least of its evils is that it distracts man from the remembrance and love of Allâh. Whoever is distracted by his wealth is a loser. If the heart is distracted from the remembrance of Allâh, then shaytan takes up residence in it and directs it towards whatever he wishes. When shaytan makes a heart familiar with the ways of evil, he prompts it to do a few good deeds in order to delude its owner into thinking that he is, on the whole, a doer of good.

Ibn Mas'ud said, "Each and every person in this world is like a guest and his wealth is only on loan. The guest leaves and the loan is eventually repaid."

It has been said that love for the life of this world is the root of all evils, for it ruins people's faith in so many ways: First, love for it leads to over emphasizing its importance when it is insignificant in the sight of Allâh. It is one of the greatest wrong actions to attach importance to what Allâh considers trivial.

Second, Allâh has condemned it. He dislikes and dis- approves of it, except for whatever it contains that is duly His. Whoever loves what Allâh condemns, dislikes and disapproves of, has left himself open to confusion and temptation, as well as to His disapproval and anger.

Third, a person who loves this world makes the pleasures and achievements of this life his goal. In order to ac- quire them he will utilize the very ways and means which in fact Allâh has provided for him in order to lead to Him and to the akhira. Such a person rebels against what Allâh intended him to strive to achieve: he makes the means an end in itself, and uses the means that should lead to the akhira to acquire the pleasures of this world.

This is a complete perversion of what these means were intended for, which indicates a most perverted heart. Allâh, the Most Exalted, says: As for whoever desires the life of this world and its glitter, We shall repay them for what they did in it, and in this they will not be wronged. These are the ones for whom there is nothing in the next world but the Fire; whatever they attempt in it is in vain, and everything they used to do is wasted.

There are many ahadith to this effect. One of them was transmitted by Abu Huraira who said, "I heard the Messenger of Allâh, and may Allâh bless him and grant him peace, say, 'The first of men to be judged on the Day of Judgment will be a man who died as a martyr. He will be brought forward and Allâh will ask him to recount His blessings, and so he will recount them. Allâh will say, "What did you used to do?" The man will say, "I fought for You until I died a martyr." Allâh will say, "You have told a lie. You fought so that you would be called a brave warrior, and so you were called." Orders will be given against him and he will be dragged face downwards and thrown into the Fire.

'Then a man will be brought forward who acquired knowledge and passed it on, and who recited the Quran. He will be brought before Allâh Who will ask him to re-count His blessings, and so he will recount them. Then Allâh will ask, "What did you used to do?" He will say, "I acquired knowledge and passed it on, and I recited the Quran, seeking Your pleasure." Allâh will say, "You have told a lie. You acquired knowledge so that you would be called a scholar, and you recited the Quran so that it might be said that you were a qari, and so you were called." Then orders will be given against him and he will be dragged face downwards and thrown into the Fire.

'Then a man will be brought forward whom Allâh had made abundantly rich and to whom He had granted every kind of wealth. He will be brought forward and Allâh will ask him to recount his blessings, and so he will recount them. Then Allâh will ask, "What did you used to do?" He will say, "spent money in every way in which You wished it to be spent." Allâh will say, "You are lying.

You did this so that it might be said that you were a generous man, and so it was said." Then Allâh will give the order and he will be dragged face downwards and thrown into the Fire.""

In this hadith we can see how it was love for the life of this world that deprived these three people of reward and rendered their actions worthless, making them the first to enter the Fire.

Fourth, love for the life of this world also makes the servant become preoccupied with it and prevents him from undertaking actions which would benefit him in the next world. There are many different kinds of people in this category: there are those whose preoccupation with this life distracts them from Islam and its laws altogether; those who are distracted from many of their religious du- ties; those who are distracted from any duty that hinders their plans and schemes to acquire it; those who are distracted from fulfilling their religious obligations at the right times and in the right manner, thereby wasting their time and neglecting their duties; those whose hearts are too preoccupied with this life to be able to give their full attention to their worship when they fulfil their religious duties; and those whose hearts are not devoted to Allâh, so that their fulfilling these duties is only an outward show without any inward sincerity and these are the least common type from amongst the lovers of this life.

A less extreme form of love for the life of this world is that in which it simply distracts the servant from his true source of happiness: which is to dedicate his heart to the love of his Lord, and his tongue to remembering Him. Love for and obsession with the life of this world inevitably limit the servant's chances in the next world, in the same way that love for the next world limits his life in this world.

Fifth, love for the life of this world makes it the servant's chief preoccupation. Anas Ibn Malik, may Allâh be pleased with him, reported that the Messenger of Allâh: said, "Whoever is preoccupied with the next life, Allâh will place his wealth within his heart, and gather his people around him, so that life will come and offer itself to him. Whoever is preoccupied with this life, Allâh will make his poverty apparent in his eyes, and scatter his people from around him, and only what has been written for him in this world will come to him."

Sixth, the one who loves the life of this world the most is the one who suffers from it the most. His suffering is of three kinds: his suffering in this life itself as a result of his striving to achieve worldly gains and his competing with its people over them; his suffering in the barzakh because he missed out in this life and regrets his lost opportunities for now he is on his way to meet Allâh in such a state that he wishes he will never meet Him; and his suffering because he did not succeed in finding a substitute for Him in this life. Such a man suffers the most severe torment in the grave as sorrow, grief and regret all eat away at his soul, just in the same way as the worms who are eating away at his body.

To summarize, the one who loves the life of this world suffers in this world, in his grave, and on the Day that he meets his Lord. Allâh, the Most Exalted, says: So do not let their wealth and their children dazzle you. Surely Allâh intends to punish them in the life of this world through this, and they themselves will perish while they are disbelievers.

One of our righteous predecessors said about this ayah, "Allâh 'punishes them' through their striving to acquire this world; 'they will perish' as a result of their love for it; 'while they are disbelievers' because they have denied the rights which are due to Allâh in it."

Seventh, the one who loves the life of this world and prefers it to the next life is the lowest of creation and the least intelligent: he prefers illusion to reality, dreaming to being wide awake, the short-lived shade to eternal bliss, and the temporary shelter to the everlasting abode. He ex- changes his life in the akhira for one which is no more than an illusion. A life that is no more than a passing shadow cannot fool any Muslim who has an intellect.

Some of our predecessors have often quoted this verse of poetry: people who take pleasure in a world that will vanish, falling in love with a fading shadow is sheer stupidity!

Yunus Ibn Abdal-'Ala said, "To me the life of this world can be compared to a man who falls asleep, and in a dream he sees whatever he likes and whatever he dislikes, and while he is in this state, he suddenly wakes up!"

One of the things to which this life can most easily be compared is a shadow: it appears to be permanent, but in reality it is in a constant state of growing smaller or larger, and when you try to chase it and catch it, you cannot! It can also be compared to a mirage in a desert which: The thirsty one imagines is water until he reaches it and finds that it is nothing and instead of it he finds Allâh Who pays him what is due to him and Allâh is swift in the reckoning.

The life of this world can also be compared to a deformed, repulsive, old woman who is untrue and deceitful to whomever proposes to her. She dresses in all manner of adornment and beautiful attire in order to conceal her ugliness and fickleness. Her suitors, deceived by her outward appearance, eventually propose to her.

She tells them, "I want no dowry from you -except that you give up the akhira: I and the akhira are deadly enemies, and we are neither permitted nor allowed to meet each other."

The suitors, completely taken in by her words, reply, "There is no blame on those who must unite with their beloved."

When, however, they lift her veil, and her disguise is revealed, they find themselves in all sorts of difficulties. Some of them divorce her and free themselves from the burden, while others on the other hand, decide to remain with her only to end up, on the morning after the wed- ding, sad and sorrowful.

By Allâh! Her invitation invites the whole world to hurry and come not to success, but to failure and yet her admirers seek union with her day and night. They rush to join her in the darkness, only to awake the next morning demoralized and with their hopes shattered. They fall right into her trap, and she consigns them to their fate.

A person's tongue can give you the taste of his heart.

This wordly life is like a shadow. If you try to catch it, you will never be able to do so. If you turn your back towards it, it has no choice but to follow you.

Ibn Qayyim Al-Jawziyya

Chapter Twenty One

REPENTANCE

Turning away from wrong actions by turning to the Concealer of faults and the Knower of all secrets is the basis of those who travel to Him, the initial investment of those who finally profit, the first step in the quest for His Face, the key to putting right whatever is not correct, and the primary stage in the selection of those who will be brought close to Him.

The station of turning in repentance is at the beginning, in the middle, and at the end. The servant who seeks Him never abandons it. He remains in it until his death. If he moves on to another station, he takes it with him and arrives with it. Turning in repentance is the beginning of the servant and his end. Allâh, the Most Exalted, says: And turn to Allâh altogether, O you who believe, so that you may succeed.

This ayah is in a Madinan surah in which Allâh addresses the people of iman and those who have been honored from amongst His creation. He called upon them to turn in repentance to Him after they had already believed, made hijra, and fought jihad. Then He made success conditional on repentance, using the word 'may' in order to make the believers aware that they could only hope for success if they turned to Him in repentance, may Allâh make us follow in their footsteps. Allâh says: And those who do not turn in repentance are indeed wrongdoers.

He distinguishes between servants who are repentant and those who are wrongdoers, and makes no other distinction. He calls those who do not turn in repentance, wrongdoers and transgressors, and says that no one is more of a wrongdoer than such a person, because of his ignorance of his Lord and of the rights that are due to Him, as well as because of his own faults and the harmfulness of his actions.

The Prophet: said, "O people, turn in repentance to Allâh! I swear by Allâh that I turn in repentance to Him more than seventy times each day." I Repentance is the servant's turning to Allâh and his turning away from the company of those who stray away from the straight path and those who invite Allâh's anger.

There are three conditions for repentance to be valid if the wrong action is to do with what is due to Allâh, Exalted and Glorious is He: feeling regret, abandoning the wrong action, and resolving never to repeat it again.

Repentance is invalid without regret because if there is no regret for having done something wrong, then this implies that it is considered acceptable, as well as being alright to do again. The Prophet: said, "Feeling regret is a part of repentance."

Abandoning the wrong action is crucial, because repentance is meaningless if the bad deed continues to be committed.

The third condition, resolving never to repeat the wrong action again, depends in essence on the sincerity of this resolve and its honesty. Some ulama' have said that repeating the wrong action nullifies the repentance, arguing that if someone who has repented returns to the wrong action, whenever that may occur, then this shows that his repentance was false and therefore invalid. The majority, however, conclude that this is not necessarily a condition.

If the wrong action was committed against a fellow human being, then the one who repents must either put right whatever damage he has caused or make amends to the person whose rights he has infringed. The Prophet said, "Any one of you who is indebted to his brother in Islam must settle his debt today, before the time comes when there will be no money, and only good deeds and bad deeds will count."

This kind of wrong action is a transgression against two parties, each of whom have their own particular rights. The wrongdoer shows his repentance by paying his fellow human being his due, and by paying what is due to Allâh by inwardly regretting his wrong action. This regret is a private matter, between him and his Creator.

There are a number of particular types of repentance, of which we mention the following: First, the repentance for back-biting or slander, where the question arises as to whether the person who has been maligned in his absence should be informed of the repentance of the wrongdoer, and so consequently come to know about a wrong of which he would otherwise have remained oblivious.

Both the madhdhahib of Imam Abu Hanifa and Imam Malik make informing the person who has been maligned a precondition for the validity of the repentance. They rest their argument on the above mentioned hadith.

The other opinion, which is that of Ibn Taimiyya, does not consider this necessary. Instead, he judges that it is enough for the wrongdoer to repent in private to Allâh, and to speak of the person whom he has slandered in the same company as the one in which he had previously maligned him, but this time in terms which are the opposite of those which originally caused the trouble; and he must also ask Allâh to forgive him.

His argument is that if the person who has been maligned is told about it, then this brings the wrong to his attention, and only causes more trouble without achieving any good. Allâh does not make precipitating such a state of affairs permissible, let alone make it compulsory or command us to act like this.

Second, the repentance for stealing money must include the return of that money to its rightful owners. If the one who repents does not know to whom the money be- longs, or if it is not possible for the money to be returned for any other reason, then he must give away the equivalent in charity on their behalf.

On the Day of Judgment they will have the choice of either approving of his action in which case the reward for the charity goes to them or of disapproving of it and having whatever they are entitled to in it from his reward in which case the reward for the charity goes to the one who repented, for Allâh never annuls the reward for charity.

It has been related that Ibn Mas'ud, may Allâh be pleased with him, once bought a woman slave from a man. When he went to pay him, he found that the man had disappeared. Ibn Mas'ud waited in vain for the man to return, and eventually gave the money away in charity, saying, "O Allâh, this sadaqa is on that man's behalf. If he approves of this sadaqa then its reward is his, and if he does not, then the reward is mine and he receives a reward equal to my reward."

Third, what is the position of someone who receives payment for doing something haram, such as selling alcohol, singing, or making a false testimony, and who then repents while the payment is still in his possession?

One group of the ulama' say that he should return the payment to whomever gave it to him, since it still belongs to the one who made the payment because the transaction was not halal and it did not result in any halal reward from Allâh.

Another group of the ulama' say and this judgment is more correct that his repentance can only be valid if he gives away the payment in charity, for how can he return money which was spent in being disobedient to Allâh?

The same principal applies to someone whose halal and haram money become so mixed up that he is no longer able to distinguish between the two: he should give away in charity whatever amount he thinks is haram, and purify what is left. Allâh knows best.

Another question is this: When a servant turns in repentance for a wrong action, does he return to the station in which he was before he committed that wrong action?

One group of the ulama' say that he does return to the same station he was in before committing the wrong action, because repentance wipes away the wrong action completely, and it becomes as if it had never taken place.

Another group say that he does not return to the same station, arguing that since he had been moving forward before committing the wrong action, and since committing it made him go backwards, then when he repents he loses the equivalent of the distance that he could have covered in the meantime, had he not committed the wrong action!

Ibn Taimiyya said, "The correct judgment Is that some of those who repent do not return to their former station, while others move on to an even higher station and be- come better than they were before they committed the wrong action."

For example, the Prophet Daw'ud, peace be on him, was in a better station after he had turned in repentance than he was in before he committed his wrong action. Here is a metaphor to shed more light on the matter:

A traveler was making his way, feeling confident and safe, walking a while and then running a while, and then resting or sleeping. He came across a shady place, with abundant cool water and a blossoming garden, and decided to rest for a while. While he was relaxing, he was at- tacked by an enemy who seized him and tied him up. He saw destruction looming and thought that his end had come, that he would become a feast for lions and never reach his destination.

While he was in this state, troubled by thoughts of despair, his merciful and caring father suddenly appeared before him. He untied him and told him to be on his way and to be wary of the enemy which lurked in ambush along the road. He assured him that as long as he remained alert and vigilant he would not be overcome, but that if he was negligent he would once again be captured.

His father said that he would go ahead and lead him to his destination. If the traveler stayed alert and kept his presence of mind and remained prepared for his enemy, then his journey would be better than it had been before, and he would arrive more quickly. If, on the other hand, he forgot about his enemy and returned to his former state of inattention and forgetfulness, indifferent to danger and only mindful of the pleasant garden, then he would once again become an easy target.

Sincere Repentance

Allâh, Glorious and Mighty is He, says: O you who believe, tum to Allâh with sincere repentance so that your Lord may free you from your bad deeds and bring you into Gardens underneath which rivers flow, on the Day when Allâh will not disgrace the Prophet and those who believe with him.

For repentance to be true and sincere it must be free from deceit, defects and corruption. Al-Hasan al-Basri said, "It is when the servant regrets what has happened and resolves never to repeat it again." Al-Kalbi said, "It is when the servant asks for forgiveness with his tongue, feels regret in his heart, and restrains his limbs." Sa'id Ibn al-Musayyib said, "Sincere repentance is what you purify your souls with."

Ibn al-Qayytm said, "Being sincere in turning in repentance consists of three things: it must include all the wrong actions of the one who is repenting, leaving none of them aside; it must be accompanied by complete truthfulness and resolve, so that the one who repents does not hesitate or delay, but summons up all his will and determination and embarks upon it wholeheartedly; and it must be free of any impurities and faults that might taint its sincerity, so that it is inspired by fear of Allâh, hope for what He has, and dread for whatever punishment He might inflict and not by any desire to safeguard his possessions, or his family, or his social status, or his influence, or to attract people's praise or escape their blame, or to avoid being bothered by nuisances, or to satisfy his appetite for life, or because of his bankruptcy or inability to cope, or any other such ills that would affect the validity of his repentance and his sincerity towards Allâh, Mighty and Exalted is He. "The first element of sincere repentance concerns the action for which the repentance is made. The second concerns the person who repents himself. The third concerns the One to Whom he repents.

"The sincerity of the repentance means that it IS true and includes all wrong actions. There is no doubt that such turning in repentance requires, and includes, seeking forgiveness, and that it leads to all of the sins that have been committed being wiped out. It is a most excellent and perfect repentance."'

A servant's sincere turning in repentance to Allâh is guaranteed both with forgiveness from Allâh even before it takes place, and with forgiveness from Him after it is completed. In other words, the servant turns in repentance between two acts of forgiveness from Allâh which secure his salvation.

Allâh's first act of forgiveness is a permission, an inspiration and a means of assistance which lead to the servant's turning in repentance which then in turn results in more forgiveness from Allâh. The second act of forgiveness is one of acceptance and recompense. Allâh, Mighty and Glorious is He, says: (He also turned in mercy) to the three who were left behind, when the earth, for all its spaciousness, seemed narrow to them, and their own selves were constricted for them, until they realized that there is no escape from Allâh except to Him. Then He turned to them in forgiveness, so that they could turn to Him in repentance; surely Allâh is Relenting, Compassionate.

Here, Allâh, Exalted is He, informs us that His turning to them in forgiveness preceded their turning to Him in repentance, and that it was this that made it possible for them to turn in repentance in the first place. He was the cause of their turning in repentance which is part of the secret of why He is called 'al-Awwal wa 'f-Akir" the First and the Last'. It is He Who makes things possible and helps to make them happen; the cause is from Him and the consequence is from Him.

The servant is oft-repentant and Allâh is oft-Forgiving. The repentance of the servant is his turning back to His Lord after his having turned away. The forgiveness of Allâh is of two kinds, one being permission and assistance, and the other being acceptance and reward.

Repentance has a beginning and an end: Its beginning is turning to Allâh by taking the straight path which He has commanded His servants to follow:

And surely this is My straight path so follow it; and do not follow any (other) paths, lest you are separated from His path.

Its end is to return to Him on the Day that has already been decreed by taking the path which He has commanded, and which leads to His Garden. Whoever turns in repentance to Allâh in this life, Allâh will turn to him and re- ward him at the appointed Time:

Whoever turns in repentance and does good has truly turned to Allâh in true repentance.

The Subtle and Hidden Aspects of Repentance

If a sensible servant happens to commit a wrong action, there are a number of things he should take into account: First, he should consider Allâh's commands and prohibitions and conclude that it was a wrong action and admit that he has done it.

Second, he should consider Allâh's promises and warnings which will arouse fear in him and make him turn in repentance.

Third, he should consider the fact that Allâh has given him the possibility and the ability to turn in repentance, when He could have prevented him from doing wrong in the first place.

This gives him some insight into the nature of Allâh, His Names, His Attributes, His wisdom, His mercy, His tolerance and His generosity. This gives him a quality of worship of Allâh which he could never have possessed had he remained ignorant of the matters. The servant recognizes the relationship between Allâh's creation and His promises and His warnings and His Names and His Attributes, and sees that this relationship requires these Names and Attributes, and their manifestation in the creation.

This insight opens the servant up to such gardens of knowledge, and faith, and the secrets of the decree, and wisdom, that the domain of words is too limited to encompass and express them. Some of what can be said is that the servant learns about Allâh's Might, which is manifested in His decree that is, that He, Exalted and Mighty is He, decrees whatever He wishes. He also learns that through the perfection of His Might, He has decreed that the servant's heart must turn, and will be directed towards whatever He wishes, and that He comes between the servant and his own heart.

By recognizing some of the manifestations of Allâh's Might that are made apparent through His decree, he sees that he is part of an ordered, patterned creation, the control of which is in hands that are not his own. He is only safe when Allâh safeguards him, and he is only successful when Allâh gives him success. He is unimportant and in- significant, m the hands of the Mighty, the Praiseworthy.

By gaining insight into the Might manifested through His decree, the servant witnesses the fact that all perfection, praise and might is Allâh's, and that it is he himself who is the one with all the shortcomings and blameworthy qualities, full of faults, imperfections and needs. The more he perceives his own insignificance and his defects and weaknesses, the more he witnesses Allâh's might and wealth and the more aware he is that Allâh alone is perfect.

The servant learns that Allâh, Exalted is He, conceals the wrong action when it is committed even though He is all-Seeing and perfectly able, if He so wishes, to expose it. In recognizing that Allâh gives time to the wrong doer even though He could have been swift in punishment had He so wished Allâh's forbearance is revealed to the one who turns in repentance, and he gains an insight into the meanings of His Name, 'ai-Haleem, the Forbearing'.

The servant becomes acquainted with Allâh's gift of forgiveness. It is a blessing from Him. When He judges with severity, He is just and Praise-Worthy, but His forgiveness arises out of His mercy, and the servant is not en- titled to it as of right. This means that the servant should be grateful to Him, and love Him and turn to Him in repentance, recognizing and relying on His Name, 'ai-Ghaffar' 'the Often-Forgiving'.

Allâh leads His servant through the stations of humility, submission, surrender and expressing his need for assistance which are in four stages: the humility that arises out of need and poverty, which is a general attribute of all creatures; the humility of obedience and of submission, which only belongs to those who obey Him; the humility of love, for the lover is especially humble, and the degree of his humility is in direct proportion to his love; and the humility that arises as a result of disobedience and wrong action which are themselves a consequence of the poverty and need in which they result.

When all our stages are complete, humility before Allâh and submission to Him is complete and perfect. The servant realizes that Allâh's Name, 'ar-Razzaq' 'the Sustainer' necessitates what is sustained, and that His Names, 'as-Samee', al-Baseer' 'the all-Hearing. The all- Seeing', necessitate what is seen and heard.

In the same way, His Names, 'al-Ghafur, al-Afu ', at- Tatvwab' 'the Forgiving, the Effacer of wrong actions, the One Who Relents and Turns in Forgiveness', necessitate someone whom Allâh forgives, and whose wrong actions are effaced, and who is forgiven again and again. It is impossible for the servant to ignore the implications and requirements of these Names and Attributes.

This was pointed out by the most knowledgeable of all in the creation of Allâh, His Messenger, when he said, "If you did not have wrong actions, Allâh would remove you and replace you with a people who did have wrong actions, so that they could seek Allâh's forgiveness and He could grant them His forgiveness."

Anas Ibn Malik al-Ansari reported that the Messenger of Allâh said, "Allâh is more pleased with the repentance of His servant than a person riding a camel in a waterless desert who loses his camel and all his provisions of food and drink which it is carrying. Having abandoned all hope of ever finding the camel, he lies down in the shade of a tree that he happens to come across. While he is resting, he suddenly sees the camel standing right m front of him. He grasps hold of its reins and then, in sheer joy, blurts out, 'O Lord, You are my Servant and I am Your lord!' He makes this mistake out of extreme joy."

Let us assume that a person whom you love dearly has been captured by an enemy and prevented from joining you, and you know that this enemy will inflict all manner of tortures on your beloved and destroy him, and that you are far better for him than this enemy for he is someone whom you have nurtured.

Then imagine that he escapes from this enemy and comes to you without letting you know in advance, so that you are amazed to find him at your front door, praising you, and hoping for your pleasure, with his cheeks smudged with the dust from your door step. How happy would you be at his return, seeing that you had already made him yours before, approved of his closeness to you, and favored him above everyone else?

That is the feeling that you experience even though it was not you who brought him into existence and granted him your blessings. Allâh, Mighty and Glorious is He, is the One who brought His servant into existence, created him, and granted him His blessings and He likes to complete His blessings on him!

Our final wish is that you do not forget to ask Allâh for us to have truthfulness, sincerity, certainty, forgiveness, and health in this world and in the next world. We ask Allâh that we will be among those whose final du'a is: All praise is for Allâh, the Lord of the worlds.

Yours is the Glory, our Lord, and to You all praise belongs. I bear witness that there is no god but You, and I seek Your forgiveness and I turn in repentance to You.

O Allâh, forgive our sins, cover faults, put our minds at rest, protect and enlighten our hearts, facilitate our tasks, let us achieve our goals, make up for our shortcomings, and protect us from whatever we are afraid of. O the One Who is always on the lookout to extend His Kindness!

If you knew the true value of yourself, you will never allow yourself to be humiliated by committing sins.

A real man is one who fears the death of his heart, not of his body.

When Allah tests you it is never to destroy you. When He removes something in your possession it is only in order to empty your hands for an even greater gift.

There are six stages to knowledge: Firstly: Asking questions in a good manner. Secondly: Remaining quiet and listening attentively. Thirdly: Understanding well. Fourthly: Memorising. Fifthly: Teaching. Sixthly- and it is its fruit: Acting upon the knowledge and keeping to its limits.

Be sincere in your aim and you will find the support of Allaah surrounding you.

Women are one half of society which gives birth to the other half so it is as if they are the entire society.

Ibn Qayyim Al-Jawziyya

Patience is that the heart does not feel anger towards that which is destined and that the mouth does not complain.

Had Allah lifted the veil for his slave and shown him how He handles his affairs for him, and how Allah is more keen for the benefit of the slave than his own self, his heart would have melted out of the love for Allah and would have been torn to pieces out of thankfulness to Allah. Therefore if the pains of this world tire you, do not grieve. For it may be that Allah wishes to hear your voice by way of Dua'a. So pour out your desires in prostration and forget about it and know; that verily Allah does not forget it.

How strange! You lose a little from you and you cry. And your whole life is wasting and you're laughing.

If you wish to check how much you love Allah, then see how much your heart loves the Quran, and you will know the answer.

A slave stands infront of Allah on two occasions. The first during salah, and secondly on the Day of Judgment. Whoseover stands correctly in the first, the second standing will be made easier for him. And whosoever, disregards the first standing, the second standing will be extremely difficult.

Ibn Qayyim Al-Jawziyya

International Islamic Books Publishing House

www.al-Qarni.com

www.ingramcontent.com/pod-product-compliance
Lightning Source LLC
Chambersburg PA
CBHW080607170426
43209CB00007B/1354